I'm in a Leadership Role, Now What?

A Concise, Practical, No Nonsense Guide to How
College Students can Strengthen Their Leadership

BE THE LEADER THEY NEED!

- Chris

Chris Molina

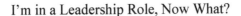

ISBN:

ISBN-13:

To Katrina. My beautiful, wonderful wife.

Thank you for everything. You mean the world to me.

TABLE OF CONTENTS

FOREWORDS

By Amy De Jong, Conner Post, Grace Lemen, and Meaghan Waldron

Find a mentor. Find someone who will help give you honest feedback. Find someone who will share their knowledge with you. Find someone who has failed and learned to do things the right way. Nine times out of ten, you will hear a speaker talk about how part of their success was because they had someone mentor them in their career and let them learn from their mistakes. If you ever met someone who knew Chris Molina, they would always have something to say about how he helped them become a better leader. I can say with absolute confidence that once you finish reading this book, you would say the same. And. You may have found yourself a mentor.

Before I tell you how I know that the advice given here works, let me put my employer hat on and tell you why it is so important. Your job as a student is to study, get good grades, join clubs, participate in case competitions... whatever it may take to be one of the few picked out of a stack of resumes to receive an internship or full-time offer. At my company, we can easily receive over 1,000 applications per job posting through our website and we usually get to see only a few hundred students at a job fair. So taking advantage of getting your foot in the door now, while as a student, is critical. So how do you stand out among your peers who take the same classes, are in the same clubs, and may or may not have boosted their GPA through easy classes or help from friends?

Let me share with you a not-so-secret secret. Now having been on the other side of the table, I can tell you that having experience as a leader makes you stand out. Not just having the position and title, but having the experiences and results to show that you were a good leader. You may not be coming out of college as a manager, but a person who practices good leadership allows those habits to permeate into their day to day actions which helps them become known as influencers and high performers (which lead to more career opportunities, raises, bonuses, better projects...etc).

The higher you climb in your career, the more important is it that you have been practicing good leadership habits. Just to give an idea of how valued leadership is and how much industries are starving for good leadership, a large IT company did research on what it meant to be an inspiring leader and found that by having leaders that were not inspiring in their organization, it made an impact of $1 Billion in lost sales per year.

So, back to Chris. I remember meeting Christopher in the Fall of my sophomore year. I was in the basement of our liberal arts building leaving a club callout when I saw a group of people dressed in suits. Christopher and a few other leaders told me they were interviewing for the professional fraternity, Alpha Kappa Psi, and they could fit me into an interview slot if I was interested. Looking back, that encounter would be where my future pivoted to where I am now.

When I was pledging to join Alpha Kappa Psi, Christopher had offered to anybody that if they would like any advice or helping with interviews, he would make himself available. I took him up on his offer, especially since the interview that I had was with USAA, a diversified financial services group and bank for many military members and their families. With his background in the Marines, I asked him to tell me a bit of about the military as well as help me with interviewing. Out of 25 students (masters students and rising seniors) interviewed, I was the youngest, least experienced, and yet one of the 12 that received an internship offer. I also became the first sophomore they ever hired in their function. I sought advice from Chris, and his advice worked. Thus started our mentorship.

My first semester officially as a brother in Alpha Kappa Psi, I wanted to contribute and take a leadership role that in the past had been a challenge to be successful, the Fundraising committee head. For one my of my first events, we decided to sell Rice Krispie treats in front of the bars and I needed volunteers to help man the booth. I remember having trouble getting people to sign-up so I started calling people individually.

"Hey Steven, are you able to sign up for a shift for our fundraising event?"

"No, I can't. Sorry," he responded.

Frustrated with the lack of interest to help our organization, I lashed back.

"Why? What are you doing instead?" Oops. I'm sure you can imagine his response.

I will be the first to admit, my first try as a leader was a fail. I was a bossy little girl that had nothing except the title of Fundraising committee head. I was upset and felt like I was the only one that cared. What was I doing wrong? What did I miss? Should I not be upset? I looked to Chris for advice.

From then on, it seemed like almost every encounter we had for the rest of the year was spent talking about what I was doing, what he learned from his experience, and what I could do better to be more effective. Sometimes he would be a sounding board for me to vent out my frustration or stress. He would just listen and then tell me that it was good that I felt frustrated because that meant that I cared, then he would give me feedback. I ended the semester with 2 successful events and a net profit. Seeing the change I had in just one semester, I became ambitious. Christopher's energy for leadership was so contagious that I now wanted to run for President in the coming election to see if I could fill his shoes. I knew that I had a lot of ground to make up within a semester to be in a position to even be considered to fill the shoes of one of the best leaders our organization had ever had.

The first thing I learned was to gain situational awareness. For the next semester, I did not take on a leadership role in Alpha Kappa Psi and instead took every opportunity to shadow Christopher and his leadership. So, I attended every executive board meeting, volunteered where I could, made every effort to get to know all the members, and spent those months focused on understanding the "Why" behind the "How" of Christopher Molina. I would see how he interacted with the other leaders in our organization, respond to challenges, and praise good work. If you ever sat in one of those meetings, you may become mesmerized in the conversations because Chris was rarely the first to give a solution or decide next steps yet he was clearly leading the group discussion. It was an art that he had mastered and was willing to share with me. Now, he is about to share it with you.

Flash forward to now, I can tell you that I was elected president after him and had a year full of challenges that let me practice the skills he taught me. That experience led to my admission to a

4

selective combined-degree program to earn my both my Bachelors and MBA in just 4.5 years, be in a position where I was President of the Society for Human Resource Management leading peers that were at least 3-4 years my senior, and winning internships with no prior full-time work experience. All because I had practiced leadership and had results to show for it.

Now, just 2 years post-graduation, I am performing among the top of my peers, leading global initiatives for our rotation program, and working in a role that consults with senior leadership (in a company that employs over 140,000 team members world-wide) to be better leaders and to drive productivity in their organizations.

It's never too soon to start building good leadership habits. If you are anxious about becoming a leader, that's good. As Chris would say, it just means that you care. ☺

- Amy

Chris Molina and I met years ago as we were both working on our Undergraduate degrees at Purdue University. Our relationship began as peers in a business related student organization and quickly developed into a deep friendship based around similar likes, dislikes, aspirations, and mutual respect. In the years I have known Chris, he has consistently displayed the leadership skills he documents within this book. Not only has he served as a primary example of these traits, but he has gone out of his way to teach others on how to properly hone them as well. Just off of the top of my head I can think of at least ten individuals, including myself, who go to Chris on a regular basis for professional and personal advice. His apt ability to assess unique situations and aid in the path to finding solutions has helped a great deal of individuals find success.

Interestingly enough, Chris is not a fan of writing. He would likely say that his most preferred form of communication is oral. In fact, years ago he began to formally use his verbal skills conducting talks and lectures to groups of young professionals. In this moment anyone around could tell that Chris had found his calling. Not only was he comfortable and highly satisfied with the work he was doing, but individuals who attended these talks raved about the content and delivery of the messages. When Chris decided to write a book, he did it with the same amount of passion, dedication, and excitement. Once I saw that, I understood that this is a subject matter which he has a great deal of passion for. Being a strong and impactful leader is something Chris has a solid comprehension of and he makes that quite clear in the chapters of this book. His understanding of the need to appeal to individuals emotionally and professionally along with the need for high levels of commitment and communication are absolute MUSTS I have found in my leadership roles over the past few years.

One of the traits which bonds Chris and I, is an enthusiasm for leadership. However, there is a distinct difference between the two of us. Early in my career, my motives were a bit more selfish. I was focused on personal success through the means of moving up in leadership roles. I had my eye on the numeric metric the team was judged against rather than the intrinsic goals of leadership including; team ownership, personal development, team functioning, and morale. Chris has always thought about the team first and this book shows exactly that. There is not a doubt in my mind that if I could have read these chapters five years ago, I would have avoided some fundamental mistakes of individuals new to leadership roles.

- Conner

We all have the same amount of hours in the day as Chris Molina. Yes, really. If you know Chris, then that can be hard to believe. And if you haven't had the opportunity to meet him, his credibility becomes quite evident early-on in this book. As to how he accomplishes everything, I do not know. Or did not know. Upon reading, "I'm in a Leadership Role, Now What?", I began piecing together the skills and attributes that make Chris the kind of leader that brings about positive change, the skills that make Chris the kind of leader you want to follow.

I don't think it was until a few years after I met Chris that I fully realized he was a mentor to me. In my eyes, Chris was just a great friend (and still is) but there were key differences between him and my other friends. Chris motivated and encouraged me. He did not solve my problems for me but instead provided the space and support for me to succeed. Chris is friends with many people, but even more significantly Chris is a leader to many people. A leader not by force or a need to control but by tried and true leadership methods developed over years of experience and education. "I'm in a Leadership Role, Now What?" is exactly the book I wish I had read as a college freshman. If Chris had written this book back then, I'm sure he would have encouraged me to read it. But I was lucky and instead I had the opportunity to see the methods outlined in the following chapters played out in real time. I had the opportunity to see the success; to even benefit from the success of Chris's leadership.

However, it would appear that Chris is not satisfied with only helping people he knows. That selflessness is why you are reading this book. An easy-to-read, unintimidating approach to the intimidating aspects of leadership, "I'm in a Leadership Role, Now What?" is the navigational guide that can turn any leadership opportunity into a platform for continued success. And I want to emphasize "continued success". Just like when Chris helped me that time when my car wouldn't start, it was five degrees out, and I had no way of getting groceries, or the time when I had no clue what I was going to do with my academic career, or the time when....well, you get it, college had its rough patches for me--this book will mentor you through your first leadership role in an extracurricular club in college and to your first leadership role as a manager at your company after college. No matter where you are starting from, "I'm in a Leadership Role, Now What?" can be a tool to take the next step.

In a world where social media has us comparing ourselves to others at an alarmingly high rate, it can be easy to look at Chris's accomplishments and compare them to your own; I'm sure we have all had moments where we looked at someone we admire and think, "How could I ever accomplish that!?". Of course, this is the opposite emotion Chris would ever want to inflict on someone. Maybe that is a reason-for I know I am not the only one who has admired what Chris has been able to accomplish-Chris wrote this book, to show people, that he was not just born a leader, but he became a leader. "I'm in a Leadership Role, Now What?" is an accumulation of well-researched methods and practices as interpreted by someone who has read them, practiced them, and benefited from them. But as humble as Chris can be, he does possess innate traits that have allowed him to overcome challenges time and time again. "I'm in a Leadership Role, Now What?" does not teach you how to be "Chris Molina". It is the support and guidance to become your own best self while utilizing the practices of successful leaders before you.

I'm writing this foreword the night before Chris asked me to have it back to him. A bad habit of mine that not even the most motivational of books could eradicate completely. A habit, I am sure, Chris is familiar with given I reported to him as the special event coordinator for the business organization we were both members of. But Chris still asked me. And like a great leader, he provided help when it came to my weak spots which is why I received a follow up email giving me a preferred timeframe for completion. I have never written a forward before and like many new challenges we are faced with, fear set in--fear of failing. Maybe Chris knew all along that when he asked me to write this, he would be placing me smack dab in the middle of the title of his book. Here I was, in, not exactly a leadership position, but an unfamiliar situation where someone was counting on me and after reading that first sentence of the email, "...looking for a good foreword...", my mind immediately jumped to, "now what?". As I finished the email and began reading "I'm in a Leadership Role, Now What?", it became more evident with each chapter why Chris had asked me and with each chapter, confidence in myself to complete this task grew.

To be a leader, a good leader, is no easy task. This is a fact I am sure Chris is aware of. However, this has never stopped him from trying. "I'm in a Leadership Role, Now What?", is the book to get you trying. Not only does it push you to take the first step, it sets you up for success on your tenth step. Will I ever be able to fully explain what makes Chris Molina a great leader? Will I ever be able to fully explain how you too can be a great leader? Probably not. But "I'm in a Leadership Role, Now What?" is the closest I've seen so far.

- Grace

"Be a leader, not a follower." For as long as I can remember, my father has said those words to me as often as he could. At a young age, they were nothing more than words. As a teenager, the were less a suggestion, and more a threat. As a young adult, they were my motivation. Now, these are words I live by. The meaning behind these words has never changed, but my interpretation of them has, very drastically.

During those aforementioned motivational years, I met Chris while joining a business organization at Purdue University. Unlike Mr. Molina, I wasn't quite ready to show the world my "lead, not follow" mentality - let's get real here, I was a college student looking to make friends, build my resume, and build a network of professional connections. While I took the backseat, Chris quickly moved into the presidential role of our incoming class. I fondly remember thinking he was a natural in the president's role. Chris took to it like a fish takes to water. Truth be told, I remember feeling a bit of envy for how easy he made it look and how quickly everyone seemed to bond with him. What I realized a bit later, after getting to know Chris more personally was two things: one, he had a few years on the rest of us, and two, he was a Marine.

After high school, I chose to go to college, to find myself through classes, organizations, and friendships. At the same age, Chris chose to join the US Marines and wage that battle within while serving this country. These very different life choices ultimately brought us both to the same place in 2011. What I was searching for in that room: friends, fun, and a side of resume building, Chris had already sought out and grasped hold of. While I believe Chris walked into that room with a better appreciation for who he was, I also believe his passion to never stop learning and developing himself brought him to this group for the same reasons.

In the years following, Chris held many titles, but the most important of which was "leader". It didn't matter if he was a General Member or the President, Chris always put the betterment of the organization as a whole above any individual need, especially his own. Chris made every person feel important. He made sure that every opinion was heard and considered. He encouraged each person to take ownership in their membership and bring forth their best effort. Chris made it so that everyone wanted to contribute to the bottom line, and not just those that held a title. During his time as president, Chris empowered those holding titles, the executive board, to take ownership of their tasks and hone new ideas. He followed up weekly on the status of our roles, offered his opinion and his help, but never did he attempt to take over these roles. Chris had faith in his executive board which in turn allowed each of them to have faith in themselves. As leader of the organization, Chris helped to build an organization of leaders.

This book was no doubt delivered to me at a pivotal time in my career. What has resonated most is that leaders exist in follower roles and great leaders also know when to follow. Often, good leaders learn most from their followers. I think exceptional leaders, extend his or her hand down the ladder, and pull new leaders up with them. What this means for you, is continue to be a student of your passions; grow loyalty to your peers and beliefs; have faith in your strengths, but also your weaknesses; and never stop listening.

So will you be a leader, or a follower?

- Meaghan

INTRODUCTION

T here are more and more people going to college than ever before, and so the advice that college students are receiving is "you need to differentiate yourself." Decades ago, simply going to college was enough to set you apart from everyone else—but not anymore. When today's college student responds to that advice by asking *how* they can differentiate themselves, the response is to "seek leadership opportunities" or "get a leadership position."

But here's the problem: Nobody is telling these students what to do once they finally get a leadership position. For the student leaders that find themselves in this position, they end up imitating examples from three places.

1. Their parents

2. Supervisors from jobs they've had

3. TV/Movies

Unfortunately, these three places often don't provide solid leadership traits or principles. Luckily for you, this book has been designed to address the common issues that young leaders encounter. This book will provide you practical, no-nonsense, proven leadership advice that will accelerate your journey to becoming a trusted leader among your peers and will help you stand out.

Why should you trust me?

→ I've had the privilege of being a non-traditional student, and, naturally, this gives me a unique perspective. Immediately after graduating high school, I enlisted in the United States Marine Corps. During my seven years in the military, I was surrounded by strong leaders every day. I was captivated by the plethora of leadership traits, principles, and examples that the Marine Corps pounded into my brain. Because of this, I absolutely *love* all things that deal with leadership. One of my ideas of fun is sitting down with an article or book about leadership to read and dissect it.

→ I attended college after I was honorably discharged from the Marine Corps, and I participated in various student organizations on campus. I was able to apply the real-life leadership traits, principles, and examples I had learned, and that helped me push our student organizations and student leaders toward success.

→ Since 2004, when I was 18 years old, I've been learning about leadership and practicing it. Learning and practicing, over and over. I've taken my lessons learned and put them in this book for you.

Many students are beginning their journey toward becoming a leader. For many of these students, this is a slow journey. Few of these students get the opportunity to be in a leadership position as a student, which means the first time they exercise their leadership "muscle" is in their early- to mid-30s (or mid- to late-20s for the über ambitious). The unfortunate reality is that most people won't pursue leadership advice or development until they are in their first role as a supervisor or manager. This is the slowest path toward becoming a good, strong leader. But you're different. You've decided to pick up this book, which means you're already ahead of your peers (before even finishing the upcoming chapters). Once you finish this book, you'll have all the tools you need to be a better leader. You'll have a solid leadership foundation, and you'll be able to set the example for other aspiring leaders to emulate.

Need proof? What better proof than feedback from people that experienced me practicing the leadership advice that I've put in this book?

> *"I've been fortunate to work with Chris while in undergrad [while we were in the same student organization]. And watching him lead our organization has taught me many things. If you want respect and admiration, you must lead with passion and dedication."*
>
> —Pradeep Gopal, Senior Digital Analyst at McKinsey & Company

> *"Following [Chris's] lead, I started looking at all the ways I was just a boss and not a leader. The advice [he] first gave me when we met led me down the path to discover the true meaning of leadership. When all I knew before were the technical aspects, I learned a more complete approach to leading after meeting [him]."*
>
> —Kyle Ruschhaupt, Materials and Planning Analyst II at Beckman Coulter

I promise that, if you read this book to completion, not only will you be a better leader on campus, but you'll also be ahead of everyone else once you graduate and enter your industry. You *will* be set apart from your competition, you *will* be promoted ahead of your peers, and people *will* naturally want to put you in leadership positions. I'm pleading with you: Please don't be the person that waits until their first supervisory role to start learning about leadership.

Also don't fall into the thinking that "leaders are born" or "I'm a natural leader." There are no "natural leaders." All leaders are forged and crafted through their experiences and what they learn from them. Just as iron ore needs to be thrown into a furnace and formed into shape so it can be made into steel for the structure of a sturdy building, leaders must take action to learn leadership traits and principles and then apply them in the real-world before they can be considered a "great" leader.

Following this book, chapter by chapter, *will* make you a better leader. All you have to do is trust the processes in this book and start applying it to your life.

Also, my promise to you is that I've done my best to make this book concise and to the point. I hate fluff and I love brevity. Strap yourself in and take my words seriously; I've chosen them deliberately for you.

CHAPTER I

70-20-10

Before we jump into the main parts of the book, we're going to take a brief look at the 70-20-10 Blended Learning Model. It's important to learn about this model because it shows where we should focus our attention as we continue to develop as leaders.

This 70-20-10 ratio comes from Morgan McMall, Michael M. Lombardo, and Robert W. Eichinger while they worked at the Center for Creative Leadership. In the mid-1990s, they surveyed nearly 200 successful executives to examine how they learned and developed. The data showed that:

70% comes from "Learning from Experiences"

20% comes from "Learning from Others"

10% comes from "Formal Learning"

70-20-10 Blended Learning Model

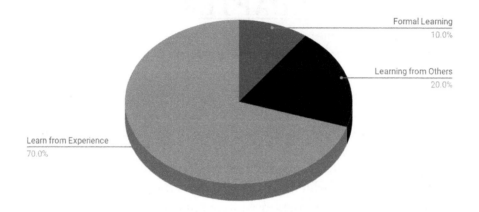

This model is tried, true, and widely used as a rule of thumb. It also seems a lot like common sense. If you want to be a professional athlete, then you must practice your sport often. If you want to be a successful entrepreneur, then you must start and run businesses. The only way a chef can make a delicious plate of food is by—you guessed it—cooking lots of food.

What does this mean for leadership? This means that you can't simply observe others and expect to be a great leader. This means that you can't read one book and expect to be a great leader (but this is a good start!). This also means that you can't expect to be a great leader by *just* being in many leadership roles. You must incorporate all three aspects of the Blended Learning Model.

Obviously, you need to focus on the biggest section of this model, "learning from experience." Now, this might sound very similar to the advice of "seek leadership opportunities," but we're not going to leave you there. In the coming chapters, we will outline how you should act once you get into those leadership roles.

CHAPTER II

Limiting Beliefs

USMC (United States Marine Corps) Leadership Principle: "Know Yourself and Seek Self-Improvement"

This principle of leadership should be developed by the use of leadership traits. Evaluate yourself by using leadership traits and determine your strengths and weaknesses.

You can improve yourself in many ways. To develop the techniques of this principle:

- Make an honest evaluation of yourself to determine your strong and weak personal qualities.

- Seek the honest opinions of your friends or superiors.

- Learn by studying the causes for the success and failures of others.

- Develop a genuine interest in people.

- Master the art of effective writing and speech.

- Have a definite plan to achieve your goal.

Strong leaders face their limiting beliefs head-on.

If you've never heard of limiting beliefs, they are exactly what they sound like. A limiting belief is a belief that limits you from doing something. Here are a few examples:

→ I'm too young.

→ I'm not a good speaker.

→ I don't have enough time.

→ I've never done that before.

"I'm too young" might stop you from trying to start a business, but in reality, your age has nothing to do with your ability to start or run a successful profit/non-profit business.

"I'm not a good speaker" might stop you from making an impressive presentation, but in reality, all it takes is practice and preparation to turn you into a good speaker.

"I don't have enough time" might stop you from pursuing a leadership position in a student organization, but in reality, you just have to focus on time management and ditch your Netflix habit for a couple of months (for example).

"I've never done that before" might stop you from ever getting started, but in reality, you don't need experience in something in order to get started. If that were the case, you would still be crawling because you were too afraid to try walking as a child.

To overcome these limiting beliefs, first think about this structure.

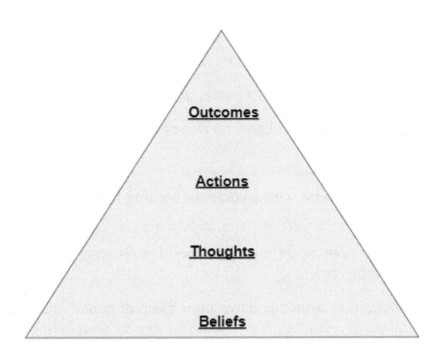

Your beliefs feed your thoughts. Your thoughts feed your actions. Your actions feed your outcomes.

Around February and March of each year, there are *tons* of people failing at their goals because they aren't trying to change their limiting beliefs. In January, the gym is packed with people, and all those new people are going to have a new body because they're "going to go to the gym more." That's their goal. They're trying to change their *outcome* by changing an *action*. Unfortunately for them, trying to change an outcome by changing an action is a *very* weak way of reaching your goal. The most powerful way to change an outcome is by changing a belief.

Here are four steps that you can take to change your limiting beliefs. I urge to you think hard and be extremely honest with yourself about your own limiting beliefs.

1. Write down your limiting beliefs.

2. Acknowledge that these are *beliefs*, not *truths*.

3. Do a 180 and take on a new _enabling_ belief.

4. Take actions that align with that new belief.

Let's try this exercise with a common limiting belief for budding leaders.

People won't take me seriously because I'm (young, old, female, male, fat, thin, etc.).

1. Write that sentence down on a piece of paper. Writing it down and reading it is a powerful step in overcoming your issue.

2. Sit back and acknowledge that this is only a belief and *not* a truth. There are people around the globe that are young, old, female, male, fat, and thin, and they are taken seriously. If they are just like you, and they are respected, then you can be taken seriously.

3. Write down a new sentence. "People will take me seriously, regardless of my attributes, as long as I properly prepare and present myself in the proper manner."

4. Start performing and acting in ways that align with your new belief. This can include focusing on how you communicate your ideas to others, changing your tone when you're discussing a serious matter, and learning more about emotional intelligence. Also, logically think through your ideas before presenting them to others.

If you can address your limiting beliefs head-on, then you'll begin to realize that the events of our lives don't control our lives, our decisions do. Decide to address your limiting beliefs.

CHAPTER III

Leadership 101

Finally, we're at the main part of this book. This chapter is the main reason you are reading this book. The leadership topics that you're about to read are foundational leadership principles and traits. The same way that a builder must lay a solid foundation before building a house (assuming the builder wants the house to be strong and last a long time), so must a leader have a solid foundation of leadership before they can effectively lead others.

You're going to notice that I describe each topic and then provide personal stories in which each leadership topic has been relevant in my life as a student.

Situational Awareness

Description

The first task for any good leader is to understand the situation. If you get the opportunity to observe any seasoned leader when they enter a new leadership role, you'll notice that they all have a "feeling out" phase. This is a duration of time where they are downloading all the information around them. They do this so they have a solid foundational understanding of their situation. Successful leaders will always study situations so they can develop a clear picture of what is happening, how it got that way, and how it might develop further. This also includes gaining an understanding of all things outside of your organization that affect your group (and, if applicable, other competing organizations). Fully understanding the components that make up your situation will aid you in developing increased situational awareness.

Because you've gained a solid understanding of the situation, you will be able to form a mental image of how your semester and school year should go. This will help you with developing goals and will help you better adapt and improvise when needed. When developing the goals for your organization and when you're crafting your mental image of how your semester will go, ensure to create contingency plans (and be sure to develop the goals and contingency plans *with* your direct reports). These contingency plans should address what your organization will do if your plans do not go according to plan.

"The best-laid plans of mice and men often go awry."

—Robert Burns

As plans are adjusted and improvised to address changing environments, you will have to anticipate possible outcomes and the new situations that will result from those possibilities.

Increasing your situational awareness helps you make better decisions as a leader. As a leader, it's your job to make the best decision possible in environments that are likely to be constantly changing. Leaders that have developed strong situational awareness and have broad experiences can make sound decisions because they have an intuitive understanding of various circumstances, know what needs to be done, and know what can or cannot be done. This type of insight is sometimes called *coup d'oeil*, a French term meaning, literally, "stroke of the eye."

In addition to understanding the landscape involving your organization, you also need to have situational awareness in every meeting and every situation that involves you being a leader. Situational awareness, in this context, means understanding who's in the room, their moods, the dynamics of the relationships of the people in the room, any current events that might affect these people, and how that might affect their decision making. This might seem like a lot, but once you get to know your direct reports and create a genuine professional relationships, this shouldn't be difficult. We will talk more about communicating with others in the next chapter, but I think it's important to mention this vital principle here too. If you've ever observed a leader when they're lacking situational awareness in a meeting, you will notice that they seem to lack tact (and you'll notice that they're a bit ineffective with their communication as well).

Tact means that you can deal with people in a manner that will maintain good relations and avoid problems.

Lacking tact also looks a lot like someone "putting their foot in their mouth." This is important for a leader because if you can maintain good relations and avoid problems, then teamwork becomes easier, and you can seamlessly maintain good order. With constant situational awareness, future conflicts and problems will be easier to resolve because relationships have started in a good, solid place rather than a rocky place.

Application to Student Groups

My first example here is pretty simple. Before I started my term as president, I did a couple of things.

1. During my first semester in our student group, I did not take on a leadership role. I did this because I wanted to experience what it was like to just be a member. This is important because if you only experience an organization from a leadership position, then it will be easy for you lose sight of what it feels like to be a member. Personally, this experience helped me observe the group as a whole so I could gain situational awareness. On a side note, this also helped show that I was committed to our group. I showed up to all the events, I volunteered when people asked for help (and when they didn't ask), and I showed interest in all matters involving our group. These types of actions (going to events, volunteering, showing interest) are expected of leaders but not necessarily expected of members. Because of this, I was able to display my *enthusiasm* for our organization.

   Enthusiasm is defined as a sincere interest and exuberance in the performance of your duties. If you are enthusiastic, you are optimistic, cheerful, and willing to accept the challenges.

2. After that first semester, I took on various leadership roles within our group but not president. I started with a leadership role that had a small amount of responsibility, then I pursued roles with increasing responsibilities. I did this because I was sincerely interested in the roles and wanted to help move our group in a positive direction, but also because taking these roles helped me understand how our leadership group operated. I gained understanding of their norms, and I steadily gained influence because of my experience in these roles. It's also important to note that I performed my duties well within these roles. It's not enough to just *have* the role, you must perform well. Because I had held several leadership roles within our group, I could speak from experience and my opinion carried a bit more weight when I was president.

3. I always asked people about their thoughts on issues and topics regarding our group. This helped me understand various viewpoints which gave me better situational awareness.

4. As mentioned in the description, I read every single document that pertained to our group. For us, that meant national regulations, our bylaws, campus regulations, etc. That might seem daunting, but you only need to read them once, and they can help give you ideas on how to make your group better.

There were also a couple of times where I lacked situational awareness. One time in particular was in early 2014. I was on my way to my Botany 201 class, which was located at the Lilly Hall on campus. While I was walking up the stairs, I started to hear sirens blaring, seemingly coming from every direction. My phone buzzed, I reached into my pocket, pulled it out, typed my passcode, and opened my phone. There had been a school shooting/stabbing that resulted in a student dying. After seeing the alert, I took several important steps, including letting people know I was safe, making sure that everyone I knew was safe, and even reaching out to a friend who was in close proximity to the shooting/stabbing to see if he needed a friend. This happened to be my first semester as president of our student organization.

In spite of the tragedy that has just occurred, I knew that I still needed to perform my duties as president. This horrible act happened on a Tuesday, early in the day. Our student group had a weekly chapter meeting every Tuesday evening. I made the decision that we would still hold our weekly meeting that evening. I sent a message to our group. Shortly after, I received a message from Meaghan, our executive vice president, who is second in command after the president. She wanted to talk to me about our meeting. After our conversation, Meaghan helped me realize that it was a bad idea and that we should not have our weekly chapter meeting. I took her advice, canceled the meeting, and most of our members attended the vigil that took place that night.

My reason for wanting to keep our meeting that night was because, in the wake of a horrific act made by a madman, I thought we needed some normalcy. I didn't want that person to affect our student group in any way. I also think that I might've felt a little bit more numb to having violence occur around me given my time in the Marine Corps. In that situation, I displayed poor situational awareness. Fortunately, I had a good relationship with Meaghan, and she took the time to ask me how I came to that decision, explained how it might negatively impact the people in our group, and empathized with me saying, "I know that your decision is coming from a good place, but I think it's a bad idea." I'm happy she was there to guide me in that moment, and I'm glad I listened.

Own the Blame, Share the Praise

Description

If you're the type of person that is often pointing the blame at someone, then you definitely need to read this section more than once. (If you're still not convinced, then go read *Extreme Ownership* by Leif Babin and Jocko Willink. It's a great book.)

Let's first look at "own the blame." The blame for anything is always spread among multiple people. A true leader is always the first person to raise their hand to take ownership when a mistake has been made. This is because leaders know that there are numerous causes of any single action or decision. If one of the causes of a mistake was confusion, then the leader needs to be better at clearly communicating. If the problem was that someone in the organization missed a deadline, then the leader needs to help that person (and possibly others) be better at making timely decisions and keeping a schedule of important dates. It's important to understand that the blame is *always* on multiple people, including yourself, and it should start with the leader of the group. Properly owning the blame will help you garner the respect of those around you.

Seek responsibility and take responsibility for your actions.

If you've never been in a group where the "leader" is always blaming everyone else for all the problems, then consider yourself lucky. When someone in a group starts to blame others, the conditions for a negative environment are created. This type of environment makes everyone less willing to take initiative and can also lead to everyone becoming apathetic. This type of environment kills creativity, makes everyone more timid, and brings open communication to a halt. People in this group start to look at each other as the enemy. Once this type of negative, finger-pointing culture has been cultivated, the leader has failed. The only way to change this is for the leader to start owning the blame. And if you're a leader and you find yourself in this type of situation, understand that even if you start owning the blame, your group's culture won't change overnight. The same way that a large ship cannot make an immediate U-turn once it has set sail, it will take time to change the culture of your group. (The ship analogy also works when we're talking about size. The larger the ship, the longer it takes to turn around. The smaller the ship, the faster you can turn it around. This can also be applied to groups.)

Now let's look at "share the praise." The same way that multiple people are always responsible for a mistake, multiple people are also always responsible for a success. Even people that consider themselves to be "self-made" had help along the way. It's important to praise an individual publicly (especially if they did most of the work), but it's equally as important to acknowledge that it was a team effort. It's also important for the leader to share the praise because positive reinforcement is a leadership strategy that works wonders.

Positive Reinforcement: Identifying behaviors that are beneficial to the group and praise them for it. Using this strategy will help cultivate a culture that is good for your group. And not only that, but it's also effective for young adults as they start creating habits as individuals. Because true leaders care about developing those around them, positive reinforcement should be used early and often.

USMC phrase regarding praising and correcting behavior: "Praise in public, counsel in private." Create habits that are fair and impartial to those in your organization. Praise/recognize people in your organization that are deserving of it and do it promptly. Likewise, correct negative behavior quickly and appropriately when required. When you're reprimanding someone, always ensure it's done in private.

If you're having trouble sharing the praise, try changing your vocabulary first. In situations where something good has happened, try removing the word "I" from your vocabulary and replace it with "we."

I sincerely hope that you've been in a group or organization where sharing the praise is the norm. In this type of environment, people are more open, less apathetic, and less afraid to take the initiative. They often take action in the absence of orders. If you see people in an organization smiling and high-fiving frequently, they are likely in a group where the leader is owning the blame and sharing the praise, which trickles down to everyone else in the group. When the leader gives praise away to others, then more praise is generated. In this situation, the leader is creating a positive environment. Being generous with credit also helps cultivate a sense of fairness in the group.

You often see this on sports teams in which the teammates share a close bond. If you're fortunate enough to have a person in your group that is participating in college sports, observe them, and maybe ask them their opinion on this topic regarding their team. Unless that person is on a toxic team, I bet they will echo the sentiments I have shared here.

Application to Student Groups

Own the Blame:

During my time as president of a student organization, I encouraged my executive board, aka my "E-board" (who reported directly to me), to do two things when planning our events: (1) Thoroughly plan the event well in advance. (2) Be creative and think outside the box.

The E-board is the group of the officers of the student organization. These officers are responsible for providing all aspects of leadership for the student organization and are responsible for their own actions as well as the actions of the student organization and its members.

During the planning for a particular event, Devon, our VPM (vice president of membership), planned an event for a Sunday. Our E-board talked about it, Devon announced it during our weekly chapter meeting, and she ensured the event was on our shared Google calendar, which was available to all of our members. The attendance at this event was so low that we barely met quorum.

"Quorum" is the minimum number of members of an assembly or society that must be present at any of its meetings to make the proceedings of that meeting valid. For this particular meeting, the required quorum was 50 percent of our group plus one.

We had our weekly E-board meeting directly afterwards, and Devon was clearly upset. She and a few of her direct reports had put a lot of time and effort into planning and executing this event. Because a large part of our group didn't show up, we were very close to having to cancel and reschedule the event. Even more frustrating was that none of our members had communicated to her that this event conflicted with their schedule.

Since this occurred at the beginning of the semester, I wanted to nip this in the bud so that it wouldn't become a pattern in the upcoming months. In lieu of the regular format at our next chapter meeting, we decided to hold a "town hall" style meeting where I gave everyone the chance to talk about any problems or grievances they might have. In the middle of talking about these issues, I brought up the extremely low attendance of our previous event. Here is the way I approached it: "Last Sunday, we had an event, and we were extremely close to not meeting quorum. Not only did we look bad in front of the non-members in attendance, but all the people that planned this event felt like they wasted their time. Now, I've told everyone on our E-board to make sure that we plan our events thoroughly and to be creative. We talked about it, they planned it, and we talked about it some more. Just like every event, we spent lots of time trying to make this a success while catering to everyone's needs. We're obviously missing something. Please help me understand what I'm missing so we can plan events better in the future, because if almost half of our chapter isn't showing up, then we're definitely doing something wrong." As I began talking and the members of our chapter that were absent knew that I was talking about this incident, some sat up a little bit more (ready to engage me in an argument), while some slumped in their chair or put their head down (ready to ignore me because they didn't want to be lectured about the importance of attendance or how they should show up to events).

At the end of my mini-speech, I had an entire group that was very interested in trying to discover the root cause of the low attendance, and they seemed sincere in their efforts to help me understand. After we talked about the issue, the individuals in our chapter were more willing to share their concerns with the room. I credit this newfound openness to my display of owning the blame. I didn't blame the members of our chapter, and I didn't blame Devon. I asked our members to explain to me how I can be a better leader so we can avoid low event attendance.

Share the Praise:

During, and after, my time as president of the same student organization mentioned above, I was often recognized as one of the main reasons we were successful. Our metrics improved, our recruitment increased, apathy lessened, participation rose, and our members were overall happier. Although my ego loved the compliments, I wanted to ensure that everyone knew that *I* wasn't the sole contributor to our success. Our success was due to *our* participation.

In our student organization's history (and many presidents before me), there were a lot of arguments on our E-board, tons of pettiness, tribalism (where groups formed within our organization), and our organization (which is nationally known as a professional business group) was beginning to be known as a "party organization." Three to four years prior to my presidency, members began to guiding the organization to a better place. Because these efforts continued throughout the years, I was fortunate enough to come into my presidency at a time where our group had more debates (less arguments), more professionalism (less pettiness), more focus on making the organization and school better (less tribalism), and more attention directed toward developing business professionals (less focus on partying). This made my life a lot easier as president. Not to sound too narcissistic, but I did attribute *some* of our organization's success to my ability to take the leadership traits and principles I learned in the Marine Corps and adapt them to the college atmosphere. Despite the fact that I personally felt I had contributed to our success, I always played it down and explained all the other reasons that we had found success. I did my best to share the praise, and I think I also helped *set the example* (which we'll talk about later) of being humble as a leader.

Expect What You Inspect

Description

If you're frustrated when people don't perform to your standards (even if you haven't explained your standards to them), then this section is for you. If you have standards or expectations, then you need to ensure they are understood by the people you're leading. You must be clear in communicating your expectations, and you must follow up on the progress. As a leader, if there is any confusion or miscommunication, then it is your fault and your responsibility to remedy the situation. Confusion or miscommunication in an organization is often created by differing expectations between individuals. Although it would be nice if other people could automatically know your expectations, it's not realistic. If possible, a leader should lay out expectations early.

Note: *You will likely come into a leadership role and have two groups of people reporting directly to you: (1) People who just stepped into their role around the same time as you, and (2) people who were in their role prior to you assuming your role. Generally, you can lay out your expectations plainly to the people in group 1. Group 2 is likely different. The people in group 2 had a leader prior to you and are likely very familiar with the leadership style of your predecessor. In order to have a smooth transition with group 2, you should still explain your expectations to them but communicate it in a way that is more gentle by employing empathy and using your emotional intelligence. If you put yourself in their shoes, it's understandable that you might be frustrated if you're* *performing well at your position and someone comes and tells you how to do your job differently.*

Generally, the way people understand expectations is determined on where they are on a spectrum. On one side of the spectrum, you have people that understand through specific details, figures, or metrics (we'll call this group A). On the other side of the spectrum, you have people that understand through an overarching vision of what "success" looks like (we'll call this group B). For people in group A, setting expectations might sound like this: "We need to have two professional events this semester. For those two events, let's ensure we have a 15 percent increase in attendance compared to last year, and I want you to have one event planned for next semester. Ensure that you're properly delegating responsibilities to the members of your committee and that we are using the planning guide for these events. During our next meeting, ensure you have a plan and a rough understanding of what you want these events to look like." For group B, setting expectations might sound like this: "Our group is known for and is expected to have large professional events that are highly valuable to *any* student who is interested in developing themselves professionally. This semester is no different. Let's plan *great* events this semester and bring in some great speakers!" You might include the group's mission or vision statement in the conversation with group B. Properly communicating with people in both groups is vital to your organization's success. An excellent way to find out which group a person falls in is to ask the question "What are some of the goals you have this semester?" If they start talking about numbers, then you have someone that resides in group A. If they start talking about a vision, mission statement, or general grandiose plans, then they're likely in group B.

Ensure assigned tasks are understood, supervised, and accomplished.

As a leader, the strongest way to set expectations and goals is to create them *with* your direct reports. Creating the goals with them will help give them ownership of their goals and will lead to a greater likelihood of success.

Many people have found success in goal planning with the acronym SMART. The purpose of this acronym is to remember to make your goals:

S – Specific

M – Measurable

A – Attainable

R – Relevant

T – Time-bound

These goals should also be clear, simple, meaningful, and written down somewhere. Following these guidelines should ensure that miscommunication and confusion are mitigated, and expectations are not unrealistic. Throughout the semester or school year, you can check in on the progress of these goals by asking some simple questions.

→ "Is there something preventing you from achieving these goals?"

→ "Is there something outside of your control that is slowing or stopping progress?"

→ "Do you need more information about something specific?"

→ "Do you have any concerns about reaching your goals?"

Another benefit of setting expectations in this manner is that it makes future evaluations easier. If you have performance evaluations—and I strongly recommend that you do—then setting the agenda for these evaluations should be easy. Simply go over the goals and expectations that you both agreed upon. While initially setting goals and expectations at the beginning of the semester, ensure that you're forward thinking. Think about what success looks like at the end of the semester and make certain the goals align with that success.

In addition to clearly setting expectations, you *need* to inspect and follow up with them. A good rule of thumb for some leaders is to be "hands off, nose in." "Hands off" means that you're not going to micro-manage anyone (meaning that you're being less controlling). "Nose in" means that you're going to be asking questions and checking in on projects regularly. This method of being "hands off, nose in" gives the people in your organization the opportunity to be both autonomous and collaborative at the same time. If you're having a hard time being hands off, try to fully understand that being too *hands on* restricts people from developing and growing. If you're having a hard time with being nose in, try asking questions like "What do you need to achieve your goals for this semester?" "Are there any barriers you need help with?" or "How can I help?" Remember that if you're not practicing nose in, then you're not checking in, which means you're possibly allowing less-than-desirable behavior happen in your group. If you're doing this well, then you're allowing people to develop, and you're sharing information throughout your group.

"If you do not inspect on a regular basis, whatever standards you set, either for yourself or your unit, are meaningless."

—General Neller

Creating an environment where expectations and goals are abundantly clear, where people have ownership of their goals, and where people feel free to be autonomous and collaborative results in an environment where people are inherently held accountable. This is a place of transparency, but that transparency starts at the top. You, as the leader, must be clear to your group about your goals and should ask them for their expectations, then use their expectations to set your own goals. This will also ensure that you are holding yourself accountable for the goals you set for yourself. By becoming proficient in this leadership principle, you will

→ Strengthen the foundation for teamwork

→ Deepen relationships

→ Build trust

→ Draw people to your organization (this can help with recruiting)

With social media ever more prevalent, so is transparency. On social media, we all express ourselves openly and share pictures and videos in a way that wasn't possible in previous years. And even if some posts or tweets are carefully engineered to hide some truth, we are still becoming a society that is more transparent and less secretive and private. We're now operating in a culture that has had its privacy eroded. Because of this, it's no longer seen as a virtue for organizations to be secretive. Whistleblowers and hackers are viewed as heroes, not traitors. We want groups to be inclusive, not exclusive.

Lastly, don't fall into the trap of confusing your organizational policy with your leader-follower relations. People that confuse these can often be heard saying something to the effect of "I treat everyone the same." Your organizational policy should treat everyone the same. (I.e., If you have more than four unexcused absences in a semester, then you will go on suspension.) However, your leader-follower relations should treat each person as a unique individual, because they are. (I.e., A person that grew up on a farm in the Midwest will communicate differently than a person from Hong Kong who is in America for the first time.)

Application to Student Groups

My time as president of our student organization lasted two semesters (the normal length), and I did a couple of things at the beginning of my term that, at the time, simply seemed like good things to do, but they also benefited our group in the long run. First, I read all of the documents that pertained to our group, which included national, local, and university documents (including bylaws, rules, and regulations). Reading all these documents gave me enough understanding of my boundaries that I would be less likely to create unrealistic expectations for my direct reports. Then, during our first E-board meeting at the beginning of the semester, I plainly explained my expectations by saying, "During the upcoming semester, I'm going to hold everyone accountable for two main things. One, whatever disagreements we have during this meeting, when we leave, we will have come to a decision. When we present that decision to the rest of our group, we need to be a unified front. Leave all your disagreements in this meeting. Two, I fully expect you to do your job. I don't expect you to do anyone else's job, just yours. If there is any ambiguity as to what exactly your responsibilities are, let me know ASAP so we can talk about it."

At that first meeting, and every meeting after, I carried a notebook with me. In that notebook, I had a tab for each of my direct reports (which totaled fourteen). At each E-board meeting, I would go around the room to each person and give them time to talk about what tasks or plans they had going on. When they talked about something they were planning, I would write it down on their tab and ask them for a timeline for when the task would be completed. I wrote down those tasks for each person during each meeting. During each subsequent meeting, when they spoke, if they didn't mention a task that I had written down, then I would follow up with them and ask them the status of that task. After a few weeks of me doing this (using my notebook), everyone started following up with me and stopped forgetting to provide a status update on their projects.

In the middle and at the end of the semester, we had "360 evaluations" (if you don't have them, I highly recommend that you start). These reviews involved me sitting down with each of my direct reports individually and going over three things.

1. Things I would like them to *start* doing.

2. Things I would like them to *stop* doing.

3. Things I would like them to *continue* doing.

During these reviews, we went over many of the goals we talked about at the beginning of the semester. Something was also mentioned, by a majority of my direct reports, that I wasn't expecting. They all said that they appreciated that I kept track of everyone, with my notebook, and that they enjoyed being held accountable. I had initially used my notebook to track the status of everyone's responsibilities so that I could keep my finger on the pulse of our group. In the end, my notebook actually turned into a mechanism that made everyone hold themselves accountable for the things they said.

Another reason to carry around a notebook: If you observe CEOs, presidents, directors, leaders in the military, etc. when they're in a meeting, you'll notice that they all have some way of taking notes, whether it's pen and paper, laptop or tablet, or an assistant that they tell "write that down." This is because they all know one thing: they can't remember everything. Using a notebook is a vital tool that highly successful people use throughout all industries. Everywhere you go, always have something to write with and something to write on.

Understanding that the "How" Is Just as Important as Understanding the "Why"

Description

The first memory I have from the beginning of my online journey of finding motivational videos and quotes is watching a TED talk by Simon Sinek. This video is called "Start with Why: How Great Leaders Inspire Action." It has tens of millions of views on YouTube, and rightfully so. Simon does a fantastic job of highlighting the importance of your "why" as a leader. This topic became so viral that Simon published a book by the same name. I highly recommend reading that book and watching his TED talk. He's truly inspiring and a thought-leader in the realm of leadership. If you're unfamiliar with the talk or book, I can try to sum it up with one of his quotes from the video: "People don't buy *what* you do, they buy *why* you do it." This is true, like most of his thoughts on leadership, but it ignores the *how*. Now, Simon actually doesn't completely ignore the *how*. In his book, *Start with Why*, he even admits that ". . . to hold yourself accountable to *how* you do things; that's the hardest part." Even though he briefly covers the *how* in a handful of pages, he mainly talks about "*how*-types" of people in a logistical/infrastructural nature. I don't disagree with him on what he wrote, but I want to highlight the trouble you can get yourself into if you don't treat your *how* with the same amount of importance as your *why*. [If you're reading this, Simon, (1) I'm ridiculously flattered. (2) I'm sure that I'm not purporting anything that you haven't already thought about.]

"There are two ways to build the tallest building in town. 1) Build the tallest building in town. 2) Tear down all the other buildings around you."

—Gary V

When we talk about *how*, we're talking about how you (or your group) are pursuing your goals. As previously mentioned, there are fewer and fewer secrets and more and more transparency in the world. Because of this, our *how* is becoming increasingly important. If you take a rock and throw it in a group of famous people, you're likelihood of hitting someone with a scandal in their past is ever increasing. These people did not focus on their *how*.

Now, this section should not be looked at as a "play nice" leadership principle. I fully believe people should (and I expect them to) rely on their core competencies when competing, whether on campus against other student groups, against other interns at your dream company, or out in the business world or your industry. We all should embrace our God-given talents and fully use them to our benefit (this is how we support ourselves and our families). If your student group happens to have talents that make them naturally better than the competitor, then you should embrace your victories and praise each other. If you end up "better" than your competitor because of bad-mouthing, denigration, defamation, or because you sabotaged their event or recruitment, then you need to re-evaluate your *how*. If you're trying to build the tallest building by tearing down everyone else's building, then you're only damaging your reputation and bringing everyone down.

Did you succeed in instilling discipline and camaraderie among your newest member? Good job! But did you do it through hazing and intimidation? Did you embarrass your members for the amusement of others?

Have you made, and continue to make, phenomenal movies that sell out at theaters across the globe? Great! How did you get there? Along the journey, were you misogynistic? Did you unfairly take advantage of people along the way?

If you still think that your *how* isn't very important, I would bet that you still think your reputation *is* very important. Your reputation, like your credit score, will follow you, and it's something that is difficult to build and easy to ruin. As a rule of thumb, I recommend that you sit down and think "What's the second thing someone will say about me when my name is brought up in conversation?" For example:

Student A: *Did you hear that Carrie just got the role of secretary?*

Student B: *Yeah! I'm glad she got it. I know she really wanted that position.*

Student A: *I don't actually know Carrie that well.*

Student B: *She's super nice.*

Student A: *That's good.*

Student B: *Yeah, but I don't know how well she's going to do as secretary. She's always late to her appointments and classes, and she doesn't take things very seriously.*

In that example, Student B started off saying something nice about Carrie, as we all normally do, and then started talking about Carrie's reputation. If Carrie had a good reputation, Student B probably would've said something like "I think she's going to be a good secretary. She's always on time and takes responsibility serious enough that she'll make this a priority."

What's the second thing someone will say about you?

As a leader, a good reputation will inspire people around you. Whether they are your subordinates, your peers, the general members of your group, or people who happen to observe you while you lead, you will inspire people if you can build a good reputation. Achieving this status will obviously help push your organization forward, but it will also push individuals forward in their lives as well. We all need good role models in our lives, and if you're in a leadership position, then you're likely a role model for many other people, whether you realize it or not.

Building and maintaining a good reputation is in your best interest. It doesn't take long for your reputation to precede you, and if it's positive then you will avoid any preconceived misconceptions. You might encounter situations where someone has a negative thought about you before they meet you, for reasons that have nothing to do with you. If you have built a reputation that completely contradicts that negative thought, then you have already begun establishing a reputation that accurately aligns with your character. In more serious situations, a good reputation can rescue you from slander that can lead to loss of future jobs or even lawsuits.

If you would like to focus on *how* more:

→ Instead of thinking "What's in this for me?", try thinking "How can I add value?"

→ When performing any task, think "Are we compromising our integrity?" "Am I compromising my integrity?" "Do our actions align with our core values?"

→ Think "Are we doing/saying this because of jealousy/fear?"

→ Ask yourself "Am I proud of the way we are pursuing/achieving our goals?"

Once you fully embrace focusing on the *how*, you and your group will thrive.

Application to Student Groups

When I joined the E-board, and also when I was president, I focused a lot on our *how*. A common phrase that came from our group was "We need to get our name out there more." Of course, they meant that we needed to be well known on campus. I agreed and wanted to achieve that goal in a couple of different ways.

Being that we were a professional business organization, I wanted to focus on that first. Our group hadn't planned many events, so why not try to bring motivational speakers to campus that would inform and entertain and whose content was within the realm of professional business. When I joined our group, luckily there were a few other members that felt the same way. We decided to plan one big professional event each semester that was open to the entire campus. Because this was open to everyone on our campus, it aligned with our value of being inclusive.

Our main competitor on campus was exclusive and only accepted business majors while we accepted all majors. Our first event was about entrepreneurship, our second was about being fully prepared for the job search after graduating, our third was about achieving financial success as a young person. Also important to note, we leveraged our university's funds for these events. (Most universities have a separate fund that can be used to fund campus-wide events. These events were very successful, aligned with our core values, and helped with the goal of getting our name out there.) The way we achieved this goal was not only beneficial to us, but also benefited the rest of the campus and increased our reputation on campus. I remember a person that joined our group a couple of semesters later said they were interested in joining because of our inclusiveness. I also recall members from our main competitor on campus attending some of our events.

I also tried to emphasize to our E-board that we needed to focus on making and maintaining good relations with the staff as well as the students. I knew that, just like everywhere else in the world, there are people on the university's staff that would benefit our organization by just knowing that our organization exists. I also knew, from my prior work experience, that many workers don't get thanked enough. In general, I don't think we appreciate fully the people around us, both in our personal and professional lives.

To start our journey toward being well known among the university staff, I made a goal with one of my direct reports to send thank-you cards to some of the staff each semester. I suggested that we start with some of the "gatekeepers" and unsung heroes. The first gatekeeper was the secretary to our dean. The first unsung hero was the receptionist that sat at the front of our main building. I also suggested that we personalize each card and have our entire group sign them. This act helped our staff to feel appreciated, positively reinforced their stellar performance (we only praised them if it was warranted), and kept our organization in their minds. We did this each semester, and it even resulted in those staff members referring a few students to our group for recruitment. These actions also helped get our name out there, and our *how* aligned with two of our core values: service and unity.

At our school, we had an "Executive Speaker" series where alumni were invited to come back to campus and share some of the lessons they had learned throughout their post-grad life. A couple of times each semester, the staff that was in charge of this series would reach out to all the student groups to see if they would be willing and able to meet with the speaker for thirty minutes. They were filling in the agenda for the speaker as well as providing a unique experience for the student organizations. I always jumped at the opportunity, and we generally had between four and nine members attending the meeting. This was important, in my eyes, because it offered an opportunity to our members a chance to speak to successful businessmen/women and ask for their advice. To the staff member who coordinated the event, our organization quickly became a group that she could rely on to help when our college needed assistance.

The subsequent semester, the same staff member reached out to us to assist with another event. This event was called "Spring Fest." Spring Fest was, and still is, a large campus-wide event that involves many parts of the university. Almost all of the schools in our university were involved, but the business school was not at that time. That staff member wanted us to help change that, and we were more than happy to help. We started the first event and helped to get our school's name out there. Through both of these actions, we were able to help increase the reputation of our school and our group. Our *how* here aligned with our core values of knowledge and service.

Another core value of our student organization was/is brotherhood. This can be defined as companionship and caring for each other. This seems simple enough, but *how* do we pursue brotherhood? We had multiple unfortunate instances where a member was grieving because they were losing or had just lost a family member. As a group, we sent cards and made sure to let those grieving members know that we were there for them. We treated them as you would family.

On a brighter note, when I started my term as president, I had a few general goals that I wanted to achieve. I informed our entire group (about sixty students) that I had two main goals as president. The first being that we all would land the internship or job we wanted, and the second was that we all had smiles on our faces at the end of the day. I also had a personal goal for our E-board of building camaraderie. I wanted our E-board to be a unified front and to be a tight-knit group. We didn't have to be best friends, but we needed to be supportive, encouraging, and helpful toward each other. I knew I needed to start there, because if we had broken leadership at the top, then that would trickle down to our members. I decided to start having "E-board Appreciation" each week. During our weekly E-board meeting, I would choose one E-board member, and we would put that person's back to a whiteboard. Then each of us would take turns writing a positive word(s) that reflected how we felt about that person on the board surrounding them.

We would then take a picture of that person and post it on social media with a few facts about him or her. This may seem like a small team-building event, but it's not small. Even though it's low-cost (it costs no money and about ten to fifteen minutes per week), it's has a high impact on building trust within our team and increasing motivation. Each week, our E-board was excited to see who was chosen, and once it was posted on social media, the chosen individual would receive even more praise from our group, friends, and family. This helped everyone on our E-board become more comfortable around each other from day 1, which lead to greater levels of camaraderie. Because we did this at the beginning of our E-board meetings, I found that this was a great way to start each meeting in a positive way. In this example, I accomplished my goal, and I did it in a way that helped boost everyone's self-confidence. I could've easily told them that they need to be good team members and explained why it's important, but I chose a more effective route.

Giving a compliment can help in many ways. Not only is a compliment a confidence booster for the person you're complimenting, but it can spark creativity and make people smile. In addition to this being good for them, it can also help you to grow your network, build trust, and strengthen important relationships.

Even though this was started in 2014, the tradition has evolved and continues without my presence, much to my delight. This specific tradition has even expanded to groups at other universities.

"I can live for two months on a good compliment."

—Mark Twain.

Don't Look a Gift Horse in the Mouth–Throw a Saddle on It

Description

If you've ever been on a team, then you know that the level of performance of each member will vary. You will have some high performers and some low performers. This is also the case when it comes to other aspects regarding members of the team (i.e., conduct, attendance, teamwork, etc.). A common pitfall for leaders is spending a large majority of their time focusing on the low performers, while ignoring the high performers.

If you're unfamiliar with the phrase "don't look a gift horse in the mouth," it essentially means that you should not be ungrateful when someone gives you a gift. If you're a leader and one of your direct reports is performing at a high level, it would be extremely ungrateful, and unwise, to ignore that person and devote your attention only to the lower performers. You should definitely divide your time so that you can help and assist those that aren't performing so well, but if you can focus more time on the high performers, then you will help make your organization successful in an expeditious manner, and you will help grow your high performers. After all, your duty as a leader is to help guide your organization toward their goals and to professionally build those that look up to you. Focusing more of your time on pushing the high performers will benefit your group more than focusing all your time on the low performers—although you will likely still need to dedicate some time to the low performers if they begin hindering your group.

Pushing the high performers in your group sometimes means that you'll have to spend more time with them to plan more goals, plan more events, and provide suggestions regarding execution. Other times, you might need to just give them a goal or direction and get out of their way.

Dedicating more of your time to the high performers also sends a message to your entire group. The message says that highly productive behaviors are recognized and preferred.

While I mentioned two groups (high performers and low performers), these two groups are always outnumbered by the large middle class. Many people in this middle class will remain in the middle for the duration of their time in your group, and that's okay. Every organization needs a group of general citizens that are just there to participate but not lead. Most of these middle class citizens will take the "wait and see" approach: They wait and see what actions are accepted and praised, then they will begin to act accordingly, and they will generally maintain this behavior while they are in the group.

Your actions as a leader will always send a message to everyone else, so you need to always be cognizant of that fact. This type of incentivization is sometimes explained with the "Monkey and Rope" story. As the story goes, there was a group of monkeys in a room with a rope and a banana at the top of the rope. As soon as a monkey tried to climb the rope, a hose was used to spray water on that monkey and all the monkeys in the room. This was done multiple times and after a while, the monkeys knew that it was a bad idea to try to climb the rope. Then a new monkey was let into the room. As the new monkey crept toward the rope with obvious intentions to climb it, all the other monkeys stopped the new monkey.

There are a couple of things that I will caution you about this story. First off, never use this example when you're trying to example your actions to a direct report because you'll essentially be comparing them to a primate, which is a bit insulting. Secondly, this demonstrates someone using negative actions to accomplish their goal. (I believe you will always get more bees with honey than you do with vinegar, so always lean toward positivity instead of negativity.) What the "Monkey and Rope" example does display is the power of creating a culture within a group. Relating this to "throwing a saddle on a gift horse," if you properly praise and give attention to your high performers who are behaving in favorable ways within your group, then you will begin to create a culture where everyone is striving to behave in favorable ways.

Application to Student Groups

This leadership principle is closely related to the "Own the Blame, Share the Praise" principle, specifically the part about praising. As a leader of your group, you should seek out your "gift horses" and encourage them to push themselves to higher plateaus. During a casual dinner where many of us were just hanging out, Pradeep, my VPM at that time, mentioned to my wife that he thought I was pushy. Naturally, she quickly agreed with him. When he said this, he said it with a smile; I smiled and chuckled, and then he said, "But that's a good thing because he pushes me out of my comfort zone to do things that I probably wouldn't have done otherwise." I've always been proud of being this type of leader because a different type of growth, professionally and personally, happens when you leave your comfort zone. I've always read that "there's no growth in your comfort zone, and there's no comfort in your growth zone." I'm happy if people read that quote, go outside their comfort zone, and find success, but the quote is fundamentally wrong. You can find tons of growth *in* your comfort zone. That's how experts become experts. The special growth that you find outside your comfort zone deals with your internal development of "change-coping" mechanisms, meaning you learn how to deal with change. This is important because it's not the smartest or the most intelligent who achieve the highest levels of success but those who can best manage change.

I'm still proud that I push those around me to be better, and it's your job as a leader to do the same. You also shouldn't be afraid of encouraging those around you because soft handling can make even the most motivated people turn complacent. Encourage your high performers to do even more, and when you're pushing them, be sure that you're communicating properly and effectively (we'll talk more about that in the next chapter).

It's not the smartest or the most intelligent who achieve the highest levels of success, but those who can best manage change.

In the description of this leadership principle, I mentioned that you're sometimes going to need to give your high performer a goal and get out of their way. This is important not only because most high performers don't need to be micro-managed but also because you don't want to waste your time. During my time as president, our fundraising chairperson requested a meeting with me. During the meeting, she went over a few of her plans and then mentioned a problem that she was having. One of the people on her committee was not enthused about any of the plans that she had and was very focused on a plan that he had. She had tried to convince him otherwise, but she hadn't succeeded and wanted my advice on the issue. After thinking about it for a minute, I asked her, "So, what would be the harm of letting him execute his plan?" She accepted that there weren't any problems with letting him proceed with his plan. However, she was worried that he might think he could always get his way after that. I told her that she needed to stand her ground afterwards, and that I would have her back. I also mentioned that once she gave him this small "win," that he'd be easier to work with. Sometimes you need to let other people think that they have won a small battle before they are willing to "go with the flow." This is important to remember because sometimes your high performers can be a bit stubborn. This is also a great lesson in delegating, which is another leadership principle we'll talk about later in this chapter.

Be the Optimist

Description

At this point, I think you've noticed a theme regarding your effect on your organization as a leader. Your actions, your words, your non-verbal cues—they all send ripples through your group. This is why it's vital for you to be the *optimist* for your group. Even if you're tempering someone's excitement because you think they have a bad idea, even if you're providing unwanted but necessary feedback, even if you're uttering unwelcomed truths, you still need to be genuinely optimistic and upbeat. This type of thinking is an important part of executive presence. If you've ever met someone from the C-suite or D-suite of a company (CEOs, directors, etc.), then you likely left that interaction feeling good (this is also true of good recruiters). That's because good leaders do their best to leave every conversation on a high note. That doesn't mean that once you've hit a positive part of the conversation that you immediately leave (that's just rude). It means that you need to display sincere interest and exuberance when communicating with others. A leader that leads with optimism and enthusiasm encourages those around them.

Maintaining this type of optimism will help develop a will to persevere among your group, which is important for everyone's development. If you remember the 70-20-10 Blended Learning Model, you'll remember that 70 percent was attributed to "learning from experiences." In the original study, the 70 percent of learning came from working through challenging assignments. It's common for people and groups to avoid difficult tasks and gravitate toward the easier path. If you lead your organization with optimism in the face of taxing, hard, or arduous situations, then you're imparting confidence among the people in your group.

If you continue to be the optimist, then you will make confidence and enthusiasm a knee-jerk reaction when your team is faced with a tough assignment.

This also involves being genuinely optimistic about all the things that might annoy and frustrate most people. Does your leadership group have a very early meeting scheduled with the Office of the Provost about a serious topic? Did a critical event for your group just get canceled because the venue had complications? Did someone forget to submit an important form, so now your group is facing disciplinary action, and you now have to fix the situation? In all of these situations, a good leader is the optimist. This doesn't mean that you're delusional and should be thinking "this isn't serious" or "nothing bad will ever happen to us." A good leader realistically assesses the situation and begins to lead everyone down the path that has the most favorable resolution. Remember: Being an optimist and being realistic are not mutually exclusive.

Not only does being the optimist help your group, but it also helps you. Maintaining enthusiasm, even when you're doing something that you don't want to do, builds your character and your resolve. This is especially apropos when you, and/or your group, have missed a goal. Instead of sulking or blaming others when you or your group is facing failure, a good leader will maintain a positive outlook while retrospectively analyzing the situation so they can learn from it and its root cause. If you remember one thing from this leadership principle, remember the phrase "you either win, or you learn." Just make sure to keep your optimism even when you're learning. It's easy to be optimistic when you're winning.

"Too often we just look at these glistening successes. Behind them in many, many cases is failure along the way, and that

doesn't get put into the Wikipedia story or the bio. Yet those failures teach you every bit as much as the successes."

—Adm. Mike Mullen

Application to Student Groups

Often, being an optimist requires you to redirect focus on finding a solution instead of worrying about all the bad things that might happen or who's to blame. On a specific occasion while I was president, my vice president of finance (VPF) came to me in a bit of a frantic state. One of the VPF's main jobs was to keep track of credits and debits that went to and from our national fraternity headquarters. Not only was this important for the obvious reason of ensuring that we didn't get in trouble for not paying our membership and pledge dues, but this also played an important part in our Annual Chapter Report (ACR). Our ACR was an evaluation tool which was used to measure our success as a chapter, and it included a requirement for each chapter to have their accounts balanced by a certain date. Our VPF was pretty nervous because we hadn't received any of the invoices that were needed to balance our accounts, and our deadline was quickly approaching. Having been on our E-board for multiple semesters at this point, I automatically knew that we would not be able to meet the deadline, and that this would make us drop our "level of success" regarding the ACR. Instead of reprimanding and going over all the negative repercussions, I said to him, "Let's figure this out together. Let's start at the beginning. What exactly do we need?" To make a long story short, the missing invoices (which turned out to be many) were in the spam folder of the VPF's email. Even though our group was negatively affected by the VPF's actions, I chose to refocus our energy on finding a solution as well as a way to ensure that our successors wouldn't make the same mistake we did. This was an opportunity for us to learn and make progress. Later in the semester during our 360 evaluation, it was mentioned that the VPF appreciated how I dealt with the situation.

> *"A pessimist sees the difficulty in every opportunity; an optimist sees the opportunity in every difficulty."*
>
> —Winston Churchill

Being an optimist has a lot to do with the way you communicate, and we'll go over much of that in the next chapter.

Delegate!

Description

Quick definition: *delegate (verb): To assign authority or responsibility. To entrust.*

If you're reading this book, then you're either anticipating that you're going to be a leader in the near future or you're already in a leadership role. Either way, it's important to avoid a common misconception that people have about being a leader. The misconception is that you need to make all the decisions. In fact, strong leaders empower others by delegating decision making to their direct reports.

When decisiveness is a consideration regarding your leadership, there are a couple of different routes you can take. Remember that the differences below are based on where the decision is coming from. Here are the four different routes:

1. Authoritarian Route. This is where you look at a problem and make a decision without any input from others (classic one-way communication). In situations where time is of the essence and everyone is looking to you for an answer, you should use this route.

2. Informative Route. Here, timing isn't an issue; you don't have a fast-approaching deadline. Because of that, you can look at the problem, find a solution, and then present your solution to your group. After presenting your solution, you will explain how you logically reached your resolution. Then you ask for their comments and thoughts. Going down this route, you're not involving your group in the

decision-making process, but you are trying to make them feel involved because you're informing them. You can also use this route if you've made a decision that is unpopular because it gives you an opportunity to convince others that it's a good idea.

3. Inclusion Route. This is usually the most popular route among your direct reports. Here, you present the group with the problem that needs to be solved, you ask for suggestions and recommendations, everyone discusses the possible solutions, and then you make a decision. When using this route, you must be prepared to facilitate and mediate two-way communication. Make sure that you set aside enough time to go over all alternate solutions and that you give everyone a chance to speak. With this route, you are not only trying to find the best solution but you're also breeding creativity among your direct reports.

4. Delegating Route. When you take this route, you pass the decision-making process to someone else. You would use this route (1) if you want to try to develop one of your direct reports by giving them more responsibility, (2) because you're too busy to deal with the issue, or (3) because the problem falls under someone else's responsibility and not yours. It's vital when you delegate, that you make the goals, objectives, and boundaries abundantly clear. It's your job to define your intent for the goals and the decision limits. After you've made the goals and decision limits clear, then you allow them to develop and execute a plan. This should be done with minimal supervision from you.

"Don't tell people how to do things, tell them what to do and let them surprise you with their results."

—General George S. Patton

One reason I'm highlighting delegating is because I believe this route is both under- and misused. Delegating is underused because of the misconception that I mentioned earlier (thinking that a leader must make all the decisions) and because I've seen new leaders make this mistake many times. If you're the type of person that can be considered a perfectionist or if you feel like you always need to be in control of situations, then you need to focus on relinquishing some of your decision-making power. This is important because there are many benefits to delegating. I'll highlight a few.

Delegating helps you develop a sense of responsibility among your direct reports. If you can assign a task to someone and give them the authority to make decisions toward resolving that task, then you will begin to build mutual confidence and respect between you and your direct report. This type of action from you will send a message to your group that says "taking the initiative and giving wholehearted cooperation toward solving problems are acceptable and desirable attitudes." If you never delegate, you will be sending a message that says "I have little to no faith in the abilities of anyone in my group and I don't trust them."

Delegating also helps you avoid decision fatigue. Social psychologist Roy F. Baumeister coined the term "decision fatigue" after conducting experiments which showed that putting effort toward making decisions depletes a finite resource that we have in our brains. When you continue to exhaust this psychological resource, you begin to increase the likelihood that you will make poor decisions. Have you ever had a very long day that was emotionally draining? A day full of stress, cramming for exams, and/or tough decision making? At the end of the day, you might think about getting fast food that is unhealthy or make an uncharacteristically angry post/tweet/reply on social media, *or* you might make poor decisions that negatively affect your group. These irrational or poor decisions can be attributed to your body's fight-or-flight response (which involves your body generating extra cortisol), but it's also caused by decision fatigue.

> **Good news:** *Over time you will become better and quicker at making critical decisions. Because of this, you will use fewer mental resources when making those decisions. Bad news: Gaining this expertise will take years. You must be careful once you gain this expertise. Just because you know the correct decision from past experience, that doesn't mean that you should quickly intercept someone else's decision-making process to provide your thoughts. Let them go through their decision-making process before you lend your advice. An example: Let's say that you planned and executed an event a couple of semesters ago, and the results were unfavorable or less than favorable. You hear a new member starting to suggest that your group should plan a similar event this semester. You, as a good leader, should not interrupt the conversation and say something like "We tried that and it didn't work." Not only is that plain rude, but shutting down the conversation like that also shuts down creativity and collaboration within your group. Instead of abruptly ending event-ideation in that way, let the conversation resolve of its own volition, then politely raise your hand and offer your advice.*

To ensure you're not misusing the action of delegating, you're going to want to avoid some common pitfalls.

→ When you delegate, avoid over-supervision at all costs. Not only is micromanaging annoying for your direct reports, it halts their leadership development, stifles creativity, and increases your workload.

→ After delegating, remember to *check in* with your direct reports at certain milestones instead of constantly *checking on* them. Checking *in* sounds like this: "What can I do to help you get this project done?" or "Is anything getting in your way?" or "How's the project going?" Checking *on* sounds like this: " Have you completed the planning for the event yet?" "Can you cc me on all your emails for this project?" "That's not how I would do it."

→ Give advice and assistance freely *when it is requested* by your subordinates. Don't hoard information, but also don't force your thoughts on other people. There is a fine line that you must walk.

→ Avoid publicly criticizing or condemning your direct reports. Let everyone in your group know that you will accept honest errors without punishment in return; teach from these mistakes by providing constructive guidance.

→ Don't delegate all your tasks. Weak leaders are the ones that are known to delegate all their work to someone else. They are looked at as lazy and not many people want to work for them.

→ Ensure that you don't overburden your direct reports. In the "don't look a gift horse in the mouth, throw a saddle on it" leadership principle, I encouraged you to give your high performers more responsibility, but even overachievers have limits. And at the college level, these students might not be able to recognize when they're being overwhelmed.

It's your responsibility to check in and see if they can handle another task or not.

Delegating is a powerful leadership action that, when done properly, will develop you and everyone else in your group. If you start exercising your delegating "muscle" now, you will be far ahead of your peers. One of the most difficult transitions in the every industry is moving from an *individual contributor* role to *manager of people* role (in other words, moving from *doing* to *leading*). A big part of leading is knowing when and how to delegate.

Application to Student Groups

When I would give direction to my direct reports, I would often say, "These are the goals that you need to accomplish for the semester. I can help if you need assistance getting started, but I want you to make the decisions. I want you to figure out how you achieve this goal." Specifically, I recall scheduling a meeting between some of the leaders in our group and the dean of our business school. We had a great conversation, and toward the end of the meeting I proposed that we could help start a "Dean's Speaker" series that would include our dean and other topic experts speaking to an audience of students. We could market it to the entire campus, and it would be a great chance for all parties involved to benefit. The dean agreed, and I assembled an ad hoc "special events" team to plan the event. With this project, I provided a vision of what I thought it should look like, then we all came to a collective decision on the specifics of the future event. Then I delegated tasks to each member to ensure we accomplished our goals. I made it very clear that we all need to focus on our own tasks, but if you need some assistance then you should let someone know. I scheduled a few meetings to update each other on our progress. We started planning during the spring semester for the event to take place in the upcoming fall semester. We successfully planned a majority of the logistics and activities needed to ensure it would be a success.

Shortly after the fall semester began, the dean resigned from his position. This new situation completely changed the plans we had for the event. I held a meeting with the special events team, explained the situation, then asked, "What do you guys think we should do now?" Everyone provided their thoughts, and we all decided to move forward with the event, despite the need for additional work from everyone. Then I delegated the additional tasks to each member, and in the end, we executed a successful event, and the members of that ad hoc team grew professionally. While our group already had a "professional events" team, I specifically chose to not overburden them because they already had a full schedule. Here I was able to use various forms of delegation at appropriate times, and because of that we all grew.

There was another situation where my director of funds explained her proposed solution to an issue she was having. I told her that her solution could work and provided a few small adjustments that could make it work better. All the while, I knew there was a better solution, but she didn't ask me for my thoughts. Fifteen minutes later, she thought of the better solution herself and explained it to me with genuine excitement. This is a good example of having the patience to sit back and let other people discover solutions for themselves. If I hadn't, then I would've robbed her of the learning experience.

You Must Be a Good Follower to Be a Good Leader

Description

It's better to be a leader in a follower role than to be a follower in a leadership role.

There is another misconception that I urge you to avoid. As I mentioned in the introduction, the unfortunate reality is that many people don't begin trying to become better leaders until they get their first supervisor role. A common thought for many is "I'll learn more about leadership when I get a leadership role, otherwise I don't need to develop those skills." Other people don't even think about developing their leadership skills at all.

The reality is that an important part of being a good leader is being a good follower.

Being a good and/or strong leader is a dynamic pursuit where true leaders are always operating as both a leader and a follower. Effective leaders set a good example of followership, not just leadership, for their subordinates to observe and duplicate. Direct reports watching the example of their leader can only be expected to exhibit the same degree of "followership" they observe. Be careful to never operate in the "Do as I say, not as I do" model. This could set the stage for a double standard which will compromise your position as a leader and frustrate the follower.

It is impossible to be an effective leader without completely understanding what it means to be a follower.

Followership is an integral part of a leader's philosophy. This is a crucial element of leadership because, when done properly, followership sets aside a leader's ego in pursuit of the organization's success.

Developing your followership does not mean that you're learning how to be a better robot so you can follow orders better. Developing your followership means that you know when to set aside your ego and listen, regardless if you're dealing with a direct report or your boss. Being a good follower means that are always aware of your surroundings (the people, situations, etc.), and you recognize everyone's goals, tendencies, and attitudes. Being actively and acutely aware of your surroundings will help you anticipate problems and possible solutions which will help push your group forward. The best way to develop your followership, which is the typical starting point for most, is to become an individual contributor and take your roles and responsibilities seriously. Be the best individual contributor that you can be. Even if you've been thrust into a leadership role without the chance to develop your followership skills in the typical way, you can still strive to demonstrate the followership traits and principles below. (I'll give an example in the "Application to Student Groups" section that follows.)

→ Be loyal, dependable, and dedicated in upholding and performing your responsibilities to the best of your ability, in regards to your direct reports and director manager(s). Always support your direct reports and direct manager(s).

→ Exude a work ethic that embodies the virtues of collaboration, cooperation, and interdependence. Be a team player.

Complete your tasks with maximum effort. If you put little care into a task, you will appear incompetent and inept.

Anything worth doing is worth overdoing.

→ Maintain a thirst for learning. Always be willing to learn from others.

→ Show pride in being a part of your organization.

→ Be a good listener. Don't listen to others in the anticipation of replying, listen to understand. The path to being an effective listener aligns with practicing your listening skills (might sound weird, but it's true).

→ Ask questions. Focus on being interested in what other people have to say. Also ask questions to better understand how you can be a better follower.

→ Volunteer for unpopular tasks. If there's something that needs to be done, and nobody wants to do it, raise your hand and volunteer.

→ Encourage those around you. This helps team building, innovation, and initiative.

→ Serve those around. Serve your peers, your direct reports, and your supervisor(s). The philosophy of "servant leadership" is popular for a reason: it's effective.

→ Set a positive example, even when you don't think anyone is watching.

You will make an impact on those around you, regardless of your title, if you're consistently demonstrating selfless dedication to helping move people, ideas, and groups forward. Setting this type of example will breed a culture that is naturally successful, and you will find that exhibiting these followership traits will make others view you as a strong leader.

The saying "Too many chiefs and not enough Indians" refers to situations where people think there are too many leaders and not enough followers. This saying does not make sense because true leaders know when to follow. If you can't set your ego aside and follow, then you're not a leader.

Application to Student Groups

During my experiences in student groups, I held many leadership positions, from the highest role of president to lower roles such as historian. I was never directly in charge of recruitment, but I always tried my best to be a good follower when it came time to help with recruitment efforts. Whether I was president or a general member without a leadership role, I always followed the lead of the person that was leading our recruitment. I believe that, especially as president, this rubbed off on the other members, and I was able to demonstrate followership traits and principles that helped all of us work better as a team.

I strongly believe that this leadership principle is pretty simple. If someone else is solely responsible for a task, and you're participating in the accomplishment of that task, then you need to become a follower. If you do this as a leader, then you're setting an excellent example for others.

Set the Example (Lead by Example)

Description

This is the crux of solid leadership. It can be easy to read and practice these leadership principles every now and again, or whenever it suits you. But if you're practicing good leadership and professionalism only *some of the time,* then you're not being a leader. You're not setting a good example for those around you to emulate if you're inconsistent. This means that it's vitally important to be vigilant in practicing leadership traits and principles, such as the ones in this book.

There are many different formative periods that will have a strong influence on you for the rest of your life. The period between three and five years old is said to be formative because it lays the foundation for how you play, learn, speak, and behave. Your first serious romantic relationship is formative because it lays the foundation for how you love and how you interact with others on a deep level. Your college years are formative because this is likely the first time that you've begun your journey toward being a professional in a certain field or industry—and for some of you, your first time practicing leadership.

During these formative college (and sometimes high school) years, we spend lots of time following others, and because of that we tend to copy the style and methods of leaders that we interact with. Consciously, and/or subconsciously, we pick some leaders, or the specific strong points of these leaders, and we try to embody them, either at the time or at some point in the future. This means that if you're in a leadership position, you are directly and indirectly affecting everyone around you, especially at college. If you don't consistently set the example and lead by example, then you're negatively affecting your direct reports, your peers, and your supervisors. People around you, especially your direct reports, can take on your poor leadership habits just as easily as they can emulate your strong leadership habits. If you ever wonder how strong a leader is, you can tell by observing their followers. As a leader, the actions, the motivations, and the habits of your group are a direct reflection of *you*. Remember that there are no bad teams, only bad leaders. This is why your example is vital to the success of your group. You have the power to influence the future actions of others, don't misuse it. Be a positive role model because someone is always watching.

> *The role model is a living example for others to emulate. A role model must lead and teach by example. Often, role models don't even know they are role models.*

Most of the young men and women that join your student group will come with predetermined attitudes. These new members are excited, motivated, and expect to both give a lot to their new organization and receive a lot from their new organization. Their expectations are high. Too often, their expectations don't mirror reality because the leaders of their new group don't practice what they preach. The new members are let down (they lose their spark), and this can be detrimental to your group because, among other things, these new members are the future leaders of your group. If you allow them to become apathetic as new members, then you're opening the door for their standards to lower, their motivation to drop, and you allow negativity to fester. If these attitudes make their way to the future leadership of your group, then your group has a long road back to true leadership. You can fix this issue before it starts by following the advice I provided earlier in this book (in "Expect What You Inspect"), but you can also fix this by setting the example. If you're consistently setting the example for your group, then you're ensuring that expectations are the same as reality because you've created norms and customs for your group. You're also providing a good leadership example for them to emulate once they become leaders in the future. By setting the example, you instill confidence in your leadership capabilities. Nothing inspires confidence in your abilities more than your direct reports witnessing you effectively and consistently lead by example.

You also gain respect from your group when you consistently set the example. It's extremely difficult to lead or influence others if you don't have their respect. In a leadership role, respect is gained by consistently practicing strong leadership traits. Garnering respect is the first step toward *building trust,* which happens to be a cornerstone for all great leaders. Likewise, don't fall into the false belief that trust automatically comes with the title of "president," "vice president," "manager," or "supervisor." It doesn't. Without trust, it is very unlikely you will learn the unadulterated truth of what is really going on in your student group. Without trust, most members of you group won't level with you, and at best, you'll learn either non-truths or partial truths. In the worst-case scenario, some of your members will go out of their way to hoard and distort their comments because they don't trust their leader(s). A good way to build trust is to meet with your direct reports and the general members of your group, one-on-one. These one-on-one meetings will show that you care about the people in your organization (which we'll discuss in the next chapter), and it helps everyone get to know who you are. This might be a bit time-consuming, but make sure you meet with as many people as you can, as soon as you can. You should take these one-on-one meetings seriously, ensure they are not rushed, take notes, listen closely, and ask lots of questions. You should make sure that the meeting is not about you; it's about the other person and how they feel about your organization. If they criticize something about your group that happens to offend you, hide it. You are there to listen and gather information. Aside from building trust, these meetings will help you understand the thoughts and feelings of the members in your group, and you will likely collect many ideas that you can use to push your group forward. These types of meetings can take place during your own office hours. (If you're unfamiliar with office hours, these are times during the week that are completely open to the members of your group to come and talk with you about anything. You should ensure that you clear your schedule a couple of times each week to provide this opportunity.) If you're not sure how to start these meetings, make sure to prepare questions ahead of time. Here are some examples:

→ "Given the opportunity, what are two things you would change about our group?"

→ "Why did you join our group?"

→ "What's something that surprised you once you joined?"

The speed of the leader is the speed of the team. This means that the tone you set, through your actions and reactions, will trickle down to the members of your organization.

In addition to building trust, these meetings will set the example for your members to meet and build relationships with each other. Various neuroscience experiments have shown that when people build social ties within a group, their performance improves. It's also been shown that leaders who express "interest in and concern for their members' success and personal well-being" will outperform others in the quality and quantity of their work. Learn how to build trust now and you will be far ahead of your peers in the future.

Your actions at meetings (all meetings, not just one-on-ones) also have a huge impact on your group. Earlier in this book, I mentioned the importance of having something to write with and write on when going to a meeting. When it comes to setting the example, there are a few other things to remember for meetings, especially if you're the leader that has called the meeting. This goes for any meeting, whether it's a meeting that happens every week or an ad hoc meeting.

Before anything else, you need to properly prepare for your meeting. This means that you need to have a clear objective or agenda to be sure that you're not wasting everyone's time because you weren't clear on what you wanted to talk about, or worse, because you have nothing to talk about. Once you figure out your agenda, write it down. Then start thinking about how long this meeting might take. Consider adding an extra ten to fifteen minutes because you never know what might come up in the meeting. If you believe that it will take longer than one to one and a half hours, take care to send out your agenda to the people you are inviting to the meeting. This will help ensure they are prepared. Before you send the meeting notice, and possibly agenda, to the recipients, think about if the presence of recipients at the meeting is needed. If you don't ensure that only essential personnel are at the meeting, then you're likely to waste many hours *and* your meetings will start to have a poor reputation among your members, with many of them thinking "Do I even need to go to this meeting? I think I'll just skip it and make an excuse." When you're finally sending the meeting notice to everyone, set clear expectations for all in attendance, especially if you're going to be asking for feedback. When it comes time for the meeting, it's extremely important that you're on time (and a bit early). Showing up late will lead to people becoming disgruntled, and it be seen as a lack of respect for other people's time.

Once you're in the meeting, ensure you stay on topic. It's very easy to get off topic; however, if a conversation starts that is important but off topic, then use the "parking lot" method. In the parking lot method, you will draw a square on the whiteboard/pad of paper/or on your Microsoft Word document, and in that square you will write any off-topic subjects so you can return to them at a later time. Lastly, agree on the next steps that need to take place after the meeting. It's always helpful to talk about those next steps before everyone leaves.

If these meeting tactics seem obvious to you, understand they are not obvious to everyone. Many hours are wasted each day due to ineffective management of meetings. Do this properly and you will be setting an example of efficiency while learning how to have effective meetings.

During the course of being in your leadership role, there will be times when everyone looks to you for an answer or reaction to a situation that just happened. Often times, these are critical moments that will help mold the leadership brand/reputation/picture of you in the minds of your direct reports. They are curious to witness how you react under pressure and how you deal with tough situations. They will also likely act in a similar way if/when they approach similar issues. When this happens, it's vital that you remain calm. Student organizations are usually replete with people who will panic at the first sight of trouble, as this is true with most people in general. As a student leader, it's important to understand this is true among the members of your organization. Know that if you panic, they will follow. Now, that doesn't mean you should be 100 percent stoic and show no emotion at all. Verbalizing that you are disappointed with an unfavorable result that hinders your group is perfectly fine. What is not fine is verbally abusing someone, breaking objects out of anger, over-dramatizing a situation because you're unhappy, or throwing a tantrum when things don't go your way. These are not the actions of a leader. Remaining calm will keep your team calm, and calmness is needed if you want your group to remain focused on your tasks and goals. If you need help keeping your cool in tough situations, train your brain to stay focused on having a solution-focused mindset (ignoring any non-relevant issues), and remember that most plans don't work perfectly.

A lot of the time, being a good leader isn't the easiest thing to do. But if you're constantly setting the example, then you'll know that taking this difficult path is worth it if you want to be considered a good leader. Going down this path doesn't just affect those that you lead, it also affects your peers, your supervisors, and most importantly, it affects you. In essence, setting the example means that you're constantly holding yourself accountable for your own actions. This will help you remember to always do the right thing, even when you think no one is looking. Do what you say you're going to do. (Example: If you talk about everyone needing to be on time to appointments, then you *must* be on time to all your appointments.) Adhering to this principle will keep you on track to achieve your goals and inspire those around you. Someone is always watching, whether you know it or not, so make sure you're always leading by example. Acting in this way will motivate others to emulate the traits and principles that you display.

The real student leader must not only carry themselves in a professional manner, they must also create a spirit of professionalism that is unique to them. Not only is this beneficial at the college level, but it will set a foundation of professionalism that will propel you past your peers after college.

When leading by example, it's also vitally important that you always display a high level of integrity. This means that you should always do the right thing, even when you think no one is looking.

Integrity: *Demonstrating the highest standards of consistent adherence to right, legal, and ethical performance and behavior.*

Having high levels of integrity is the bedrock of all strong leaders. This is the quality that will ensure you gain and maintain a reputation of having sound moral principles and character. Honesty, trustworthiness, uprightness, rectitude—these are all attributes that come from having integrity *and* these are all attributes that are respected, revered, and common among great leaders.

Cheating or bending the rules may not have immediate ramifications for the individual, but down the road it will likely lead to dire consequences. I've heard conversations among seasoned businessmen/women and HR professionals discussing people who lack integrity, in big and small ways, and it always costs them in the end. Probably the most common overlooked problem with lacking integrity deals with small, white, or seemingly innocent lies. Take this hypothetical situation: You're president. You're sitting next to one of your VPs, we'll call that person Fred, and you are in the library talking about your student organization. Fred says that he just got a text message from a member in your group, we'll call that person Sonya. Fred said that

Sonya was thinking about joining Fred at the library. You tell Fred, "Tell Sonya that I'm not here." Now, in this situation, no matter your reason for telling Fred to lie, you just showed that being dishonest is an acceptable behavior. Even if it is a small lie, it opens the door for more/bigger lies for your VP, which will eventually trickle down to the rest of your members. This is an example of setting the wrong example for others to embody.

How we do anything, is how we do everything.

If you take care of the small things, the big things take care of themselves.

If you refrain from lying, cheating, and stealing, then your integrity will become unquestionable. As a leader, you must be morally responsible and your actions must garner enough respect that you are worthy of the highest trust and confidence among the members of your student organization.

Examples of acting with integrity include but are not limited to

→ Respecting others enough to not speak down toward anyone.

→ Acting in a mature manner even when others are acting immature.

→ Displaying dedication and dependability that aligns with your promises.

→ Trusting others.

→ Holding yourself accountable.

→ Doing the right thing, even if it's unpopular.

→ Aligning your actions with your beliefs and the beliefs of your group.

→ Defending the dignity of others if they're being attacked.

→ Giving your best effort regardless of your personal discomfort.

"A sound body is good; a sound mind is better; but a strong and clean character is better than either."

—Theodore Roosevelt

If you're having trouble setting the example, try writing down the top three most important ways that you need to set the example for others to emulate. You can also try getting an accountability buddy. An accountability buddy is someone that you will share your leadership goals with, and you will continuously check in with this buddy to ensure you remain focused.

Application to Student Groups

Early one semester during my time as president, I was walking into a building that was the location for a large recruiting event that all student groups attended. This was an important event for many student groups because this event provided a valuable source for recruitment. As I walked into the hall, Pradeep, our VPM, approached me. He began to explain that our registration was not completed, so we did not have a spot reserved for us at this event. After explaining, he paused for my response. I said, "Okay. Is this something we can fix at this moment, or do we all need to go home?" I said this with a smile and in a proactive tone (as if I was trying to find a solution). I did not have a negative, accusatory, or adversarial tone. Pradeep looked at me, surprised, and said, "Wow. I kind of expected you to be angry." I said, "Well, I mean, if our recruitment takes a hit because of this, then I'm not going to be excited about it. But, being angry doesn't help the situation." He nodded and said, "We actually will be able to get a spot at this event because they have a few vacancies." Later that semester, when we had a 360 evaluation, he mentioned that he appreciated that I didn't overreact to situations and that I had the ability to remain calm.

I also remember a conversation I had with a member of our group after I was done with my term as president (I had one semester left after my presidency until I graduated college.) We were talking about events that happened while I was president and how a few of the changes I made weren't popular with everyone. Then I was told, "Even if I disagreed with a decision you made or a direction you were taking the group, I knew you were doing it for the betterment of the group. I trusted you to do the right thing." I accredit this great compliment to my ability to lead by example while maintaining a high level of integrity. If I didn't have the reputation of always putting the advancement of our group before anything else, then I might've not been able to change some of the things that we did.

Another illustration of setting the example comes from our group's biggest competitor on campus at that time. We were a chapter of Alpha Kappa Psi (AKPsi), and our biggest competitor was Delta Sigma Pi (DSP). I had always made it a point to deal with DSP in the most professional way possible because that's the way that I would want AKPsi to be treated and also because I was hoping that if I led by example in this way, then others would follow. I don't know if my thoughts and actions on this matter directly affected Tom from DSP, but he is a perfect example of this line of thinking.

At the beginning of one semester, at one of our various callouts, someone approached me with more questions because he was interested in joining our group. At the end of our conversation, I said, "If you don't mind me asking, how did you hear about us?" I expected for him to say he saw a flyer on campus or heard about the callout on Facebook or Twitter. He said that he initially went to a DSP callout, but he soon learned that he couldn't join that group because he wasn't a business major. Then, Tom (a member of DSP) suggested that he check out AKPsi since we accept all majors. I remembered this, and the next time I saw Tom, I made it a point to shake his hand and thank him for acting in such a professional manner. I specifically told him that I wished people had that attitude more often.

I think I have stressed the importance of this leadership principle enough that I don't need to say much more. Mastering this is critical for your leadership.

You Are Now "They"

If you've been a member of a sports team, worked at a restaurant or grocery store, been a part of a community, or if you've been a student in a classroom, then you've used the term "they."

→ When's practice? *They* said it's at 8 p.m. on Thursday.

→ Did you hear?! *They* said that we get 45-minute lunch breaks now instead of 30!

→ Are you going trick-or-treating this Halloween? Yeah, but *they* said we can only do it between 6 and 8 p.m.

→ Did you hear about our Final Exam? *They* said that it's a take-home exam.

Whether you're the president or a part of the E-board or leadership team, you are now "they." This is an important and powerful thing to understand. It's important because some of the people that don't identify this as a reality tend to not treat their leadership role with the proper amount of significance. They might make decisions on a whim or based purely on emotion because they don't see the impact that those decisions might have. Understanding this is powerful because it shows you the influence you have over the members and the future of your student group. You are creating and crafting the culture and environment that will stay with the members of your group for their entire lives. It's on you to not misuse or abuse the influence and power you have. Use this opportunity to begin your leadership journey on the right path. The path of the servant leader. The path where you take leadership seriously. The path where you begin laying a solid leadership foundation in your early 20s (not in your mid-30s). The path where you look back on your years as a budding leader and smile.

"I did not learn about leadership in business school. I learned about leadership when I was 18 years old and first introduced to the United States Marine Corps, where leadership is not taught by a favored professor in a three-credit hour course. It is taught by every officer and every NCO in every minute and every hour of every day, in every action, every word, every deed, and every circumstance. And, in that experience, you are immersed in a culture of excellence that is built on a foundation of virtue and value."

—Robert J. Stevens, Chairman and Chief Executive Officer of Lockheed Martin, and United States Marine Corps Veteran

CHAPTER IV

Communication

I am never one to shy away from any debate, and I've found myself, many times, adamantly providing counterarguments when people negatively talk about "this generation." Generally, when I hear someone talk about "this generation," they are talking about Millennials or Gen Z (recently referred to as Centennials). Now, although I strongly disagree with most negative things that grumpy people have to say about "this generation," I do agree that Millennials and Gen Z might have lower communication skills than previous generations. (When I say communication, I specifically mean soft skills, people skills, and interpersonal skills. I've heard some people claim that younger people are better at IMs, texting, and emails, but that deals with being tech-savvy, not being an effective communicator—there's a difference.) It's also important to note that the reason this might be true also affects older generations (Generation X and Baby Boomers), depending on their habits.

In a book called *Alone Together*, MIT social psychologist Sherry Turkle makes the case that people today are so used to text-based communication, where they have time to gather their thoughts and precisely plan what to say and how to say it, that they are losing their ability to have spontaneous conversations. She argues that the muscles in our brain that help us with spontaneous conversation are getting less exercise in this text-and email-filled world, so our skills are declining. I agree because I've witnessed this difference when I speak to people of different generations. I've also observed that the diminishing ability to have effective, spontaneous conversations also affects overall communication.

But, why is this important to leadership? Because it's impossible to be an effective leader if you're an ineffective communicator *and* because of another unfortunate misconception.

Many people think that the best way to start proving their ability to be a good leader to their subordinates, peers, or boss is by displaying their competence, expertise, or talent. They want to show everyone that they have the necessary skills to make the right decisions, to show their academic credentials, and to show they are smart enough to be a good leader to the those that they want to lead. I call this the "fallacy of competence." This is the wrong approach to initially take. Proving your competence is important for leaders, but not initially. Studies show that people care most, initially, about whether you're concerned about their interests, about whether you're warm, and about whether you're caring—not your competence.

Although there are decades of research on this in the realm of psychology, I'd like to specifically point out the findings from social psychologist Susan Fiske and her colleagues Jun Xu, Amy Cuddy, and Peter Glick. In 2002, out of their research came the Stereotype Content Model, which talks about two different dimensions regarding impressions made from interpersonal communication: (1) Warmth and (2) Competence.

Warmth: *Caring, kindness, friendliness, or affection. Displaying warmth means that you are showing other people that you mean them no harm, your sincere intent is to help.*

Competence: *Smartness, proficiency, or mastery. Displaying competence means that you're showing other people that you have the capability to succeed at completing a challenging task, you can be relied upon to get the job done.*

I believe the graph below is a great visual depiction to help understand. The graph below shows the range of feelings that you evoke when you effectively communicate differing levels of warmth and competence.

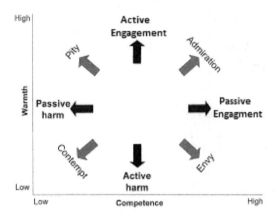

As you can see, if you do what most people do and only focus on displaying or communicating competence, then you will be eliciting contempt or envy, and you can be actively hurting your reputation among your peers, subordinates, and bosses.

People will make a decision on what they think of you before they make a decision on what they think of your message.

Warmth is the key to unlocking your leadership potential. Social psychologist Alex Todorov has studied what contributes to our "spontaneous trait inferences," or the snap judgements that we all makes when we interact with other people. Dr. Todorov's research shows that, most of the time, people initially and consistently recognize warmth during interpersonal communication, and they were able to identify warmth more reliably than identifying competence. Since warmth is closely linked to trust, and building trust is critical for strong leadership, understanding and displaying warmth is vital for every leader. Putting competence first will likely hurt your leadership because there is no foundation of trust, and without a solid foundation of trust, you will, at most, get moderate levels of cooperation and dedication from those around you.

"Nobody cares how much you know, until they know how much you care."

—Theodore Roosevelt

If you're better with lists than you are with graphs, then use the list below. I've also added a bit more information than there is on the graph. In this list, "Emotion" and "Behavior" describe the reactions you will receive from those around you (subordinates, peers, supervisors, and outside observers) when you're in the different sections.

[High] Competence / [High] Warmth

Emotion: Admiration/High-Esteem

Behavior: Active Engagement

Description: This is exactly where you want to be as a leader. You have consistently shown that you care about those around you, and that you're good at your job. When you're able to display high levels of warmth and competence, you receive admiration and active engagement from those around you. You're respected and appreciated, and other people will deliberately try to support you and your efforts. While in this quadrant, you are known and sought out by many.

[Low] Competence / [High] Warmth

Emotion: Sympathy/Pity

Behavior: Passive Engagement

Description: Here you've been able to display your warmth, but there are still questions about your ability to lead and perform. If you seem to find yourself here often, it might be the case that you have a high level of humility. Although humbleness is a very important trait for strong leaders to have, you might need to try to be more comfortable with sharing your accomplishments with others. Also, if people think you have low levels of competence, then you might need to have an honest look in the mirror and determine if you need to focus more on being better in the areas you might be lacking.

[High] Competence / [Low] Warmth

Emotion: Envy/Resent

Behavior: Passive Harm

Description: For the large amount of people that fall into the *fallacy of competence*, you will start here. This is also where lots of highly successful people start their professional careers because they haven't yet identified that warmth is just as important as competence (if not more important in some instances). Unfortunately, you will receive *passive harm* from others because you don't seem affable, and they likely don't think you have their best interests at heart. If you find yourself here, try empathizes with others: be friendly and focus on increasing your emotional intelligence (which I'll briefly mention later). Because I know many people who are reading this are in this area, we'll talk about ways you can increase your warmth later in this chapter.

[Low] Competence / [Low] Warmth

Emotion: Disregard/Contempt/Disdain

Behavior: Active Harm

Description: Here, you're making, or have already made, yourself an outcast to the group. People around you don't think you care about them or the organization, and they don't think you have the capabilities to perform your job. This is a dangerous place to be, and if you find yourself here then you probably should step away for a while and assess your situation. What can you do better? What skills do you need to work on? Is this the correct organization for you?

The unfortunate reality is that when you've found yourself in one of the less-desirable sections above, it's because of miscommunications, misunderstandings, or a failure to effectively communicate. One way that you can improve your ability to communicate is by focusing on your ability to have effective conversations.

Now, there are a couple of ways we can become better conversationalists.

One obvious way is to force yourself to speak to others on a daily basis, either through social groups or your job. I had the benefit of the Marine Corps giving me a job where I was forced to have ten to forty unique conversations every day. For about four years, I was stationed at Fort Leonard Wood, Missouri. (It was/is affectionately known at Fort Lost-in-the-Woods because there's not much to do there as far as nightlife, but I digress.) While at Fort Leonard Wood, I was in procurement, which plainly means that I purchased things for the government. I purchased anything my Marine Corps units needed that was under $3,000 with a government credit card. It was normal for me to have over sixty individual purchases in one month. And, because in the government everything is archaic (surprise!), these purchases were initiated, tracked, and receipted for over the phone. Each day, I would have five to twenty-five unique conversations over the phone with people I didn't know, and I wasn't quite sure how the conversations would go. I would also have five to fifteen unique conversations with Marines that would come into my office to inquire about their pending purchases. During those four years of doing this day-in and day-out, I cultivated a deep understanding of the ebbs and flows of a conversation. The art of talking. There I developed a deep appreciation for the joy of connecting with people and being able to make them laugh in the middle of a serious conversation. At that time, if someone could see the muscle in my brain that helped me with spontaneous conversations, they would've thought I was on steroids.

With all those conversations, I became comfortable with minor missteps in conversations. Awkward silences weren't awkward. Stumbling over my words was okay because I knew how to recover. Losing myself mid-sentence wasn't embarrassing because I had enough practice that I knew I could find my place.

Sherry Turkle gave a TED talk, and in it she mentioned an 18-year-old boy that said, "... someday, someday, but certainly not now, I'd like to learn how to have a conversation ..." This young man was using texting for absolutely everything. He had no spontaneous conversations.

Texts, emails, and IMs are just like everything else. In moderation, they are fine. But using it as your primary mode of communication can be damaging over time to your ability to effectively communicate with others. An easy solution to this problem is to have multiple conversations with other people every day, and try your best to have a variety of conversations—long, short, deep, shallow, serious, funny, highly structured, and loosely flowing. It also helps to have conversations with different types of people.

Another way you can improve your communication with others is by learning more about *emotional intelligence,* commonly known as EQ. If you haven't heard of EQ, I'm sure you've heard of IQ. IQ stands for *intelligence quotient* and is used to express a person's reasoning ability. You often hear people mention IQ when referring to how smart someone is. EQ, on the other hand, measures your ability to identify your own emotions, the emotions of others, and how you use this information to guide behavior.

I won't get into EQ too much, because that would make this book much longer, but feel free to check out the podcast episode I did with Gale Mote talking about EQ. (You should be able to find my podcast, "Professional by Choice," on your platform of choice.) During the episode, Gale talks about building trust, which I believe is one of the most important parts of EQ and team building, and she mentions the three C's of trust: Competence, Commitment, and Compassion. Be sure to check it out because leaders that understand and develop their EQ are highly successful.

Another way to improve your ability to communicate is to use the three tips, or hacks, below. And these aren't really conventional tips. All the things you learn in Speech and Communication class are still important, but these tips can help you get to the next level.

1) Use your shortcomings to build warmth and rapport.

There's a thing called the *pratfall effect,* and it is defined as "a small mistake in a domain that is totally unrelated to competence, actually leads people to *warm up* to you." Now, this would be obvious if you could see me in person, but I have a babyface. I'm in my 30s, and I often joke with people and say, "Even though I look like I'm 13, I'm actually 33." Now, when I point out that I look 13 years old, that's a small, embarrassing thing, but it has nothing to do with my speaking ability or me being a professional. That small embarrassing thing helps me *warm up* to people.

As I stated earlier, studies show that people care most, initially, about whether you're concerned about their interests, about whether you're warm, and about whether you're caring—not your competence.

2) Be strategic with your words.

There's a big difference between someone saying "You need to study or you're going to fail!" and "If you would prefer to pass your classes and graduate, then you should probably study to make sure you pass."

Here are five tips that will make you more strategic with the words you choose to use.

→ **Hesitations/fillers:** *Umm, hmm, well, you know.* Those are fillers. We hate them, I hate them, I count them when other people are talking... *But,* in interpersonal communication, using those types of fillers shows concern for others. It shows that you're willing to consider their opinion. I urge you to not fill your vocabulary with these fillers, but a well-placed *umm* can work wonders. This tactic works especially well if you're very quick-witted.

→ **Hedges:** *Kinda, sorta, maybe, probably, I think.* These build trust, respect, and warmth. I personally use the phrase "I think" very often, even if I know my statement to be 100 percent true because sometimes people don't like a person who thinks that they know everything. This will probably help you not seem like a know-it-all. (See what I did there?)

→ **Disclaimers:** *I agree with you but...,* I *think that's a really good idea, but....* My disclaimer about disclaimers is that sometimes they don't work, but, you can try them. Also, be sure to not overuse them (just like all the other tips).

→ **Intensifiers:** *Really, quite, very.* These types of words help amplify your speech. If you need help varying the types of intensifiers you're using, then grab a thesaurus or use Google. Google is your friend here. Unfortunately, I've recently noticed that lots of people tend to use the word "really." If this is you, stop this habit immediately. If you overuse the word "really," then you won't be taken seriously when you use any other intensifiers.

→ **Lastly, tag questions:** Instead of saying *Here's a good idea. . .,* and then proceeding with your thoughts, start with your idea, then at the end say, *Do you guys think this is a good plan of action?*

3) Build warmth and rapport by asking questions

A study by a social scientist named James Pennebaker went like this:

Pennebaker put a bunch of people in a room and split them into groups. He then asked them to get to know each other for fifteen minutes. After the fifteen minutes, he began to ask a series of questions to each person in each group. Through this questioning, he found out that the people that talked more felt like they knew their group the most. I'll say that again. Through this questioning he found out that the people that *talked more,* felt like they knew their group the most. Think about that. It doesn't make much sense. You can't learn more about other people by talking more than they do. In order to learn about other people, you have to listen to them. But, this was (and is still) the case. Pennebaker said, "This seems pretty simple. Most of us find that communicating our thoughts to others is a supremely enjoyable learning experience." Pennebaker called it the "Joy of Talking."

Moral of this story is that if you want someone to feel more connected to you, to leave a good impression, then let them talk. Be interested, not interesting. And if you're like me and you always find yourself talking more than the other person, then remember the acronym W.A.I.T.

Why   Am   I   Talking

You're only interesting to the point that you're interested.

And generally speaking, people who are genuinely interested in others are usually interesting themselves. Why is that? Well, it's because people who ask questions are generally more open to learning about and understanding new things. Showing interest also encourages the other person to be relaxed and share information more freely. Always try to display attentiveness by keeping good eye contact and listening actively.

Lastly, you will succeed more in having effective conversations if you *meet people at their level.* Have you ever been very excited about something, then you start talking to someone about that thing, and they are nowhere nearly as excited about it as you are? Well, the unexcited person did not meet you at your level, or anywhere near your level. Translate that to a setting where there's a leader who does not understand how to meet his or her subordinates, peers, or supervisors at their level, and you have a leader who is not communicating at his or her optimal level. This doesn't mean that you have to meet people *exactly* at their level, but if you're like me (for example) then your general demeanor is pretty stoic. When I speak with someone who is enthusiastic or animated, I don't suddenly become an exact mirror of them (that would be disingenuous). I reflect a level of excitement that I'm comfortable with. Because of this, when I share someone else's excitement, it seems very genuine. The worst thing you can do when communicating with an excited person is to show no emotion. The next worst thing you can do is show visibly fake enthusiasm. And this goes for any emotion—excitement, sadness, anger, joy, surprise, disgust. If you want to project warmth with your tone, while meeting people at their level, aim for a tone that suggests you are leveling with them. Project no facade, no fakeness. You want to let others know that they can confide in you.

When meeting someone at their level, you can even share a personal story that shows you understand where they're coming from, that you genuinely empathize with them. Just be careful to not seem like you're trying to one-up them. For example, if someone is complaining about having trouble with scheduling their classes for next semester, you can share an example of a time you had the exact same issue. You might even be able to offer some advice since you've experienced the same thing. In doing this, you will have validated their feelings, opened up a little bit of yourself to them, and you've set a congenial tone. You've met them at their level. This works favorably for bigger issues too. Let's say that your group has an upcoming change that is very unpopular. You hear people complaining about it, and as a leader, you decide to address the elephant in the room. You explain your own personal concerns and how you might dislike some of the changes. By meeting people at their level in this situation, you will begin to garner their respect, and they will likely be more open to hearing things you have to say.

In the end, if you're a poor communicator, then you're likely a subpar leader. Take this seriously and you will see your interpersonal communication work wonders for your student group and your future career.

CONCLUSION

If you've made it this far, then you're definitely serious about stepping up your game as a leader. Remember that this is not only something that will enhance your ability to lead as a student but you're also setting yourself up for success in your future career. There are students who don't take this seriously, and you'll notice that you will climb your industry's ladder faster than they do because you started now.

If you are currently a leader in a student group, remember that your group's success depends largely upon you and your ability to lead them properly. It's your job to inspire them to perform their duties. If you plan on leading your group toward success, then you must know and do certain things. You must know your job and do it well. You must know how to effectively communicate with those around you, and you must know how to set goals with your group that will achieve your combined mission or vision. You must have a solid leadership foundation that you can lean on so you know how to plan, act, and react to issues that your group will face.

You've probably noticed that your pursuit of the mastery of leadership is a pursuit of mastering human nature. You have to understand those around you and empathize with them. When you mastered leadership, that means that you have a full and in-depth understanding of the thoughts, viewpoints, emotions, aspirations, ideals, and virtues of other people. To master leadership, you must also master yourself: You must have self-awareness, humbleness, and have a genuine understanding of who you are, where you want to be, and how you plan on getting there. Although mastering leadership is close to impossible, you can get very close. To do this, you must practice leadership in different environments with different groups that have different goals.

Know that you will fail. The path of leadership is not only a lonely one, it's a path of countless failures. Although you may always try to do what you think is best, you cannot predict the future. Because of this, you will fall. And that's okay. If you think of any person that you consider successful, you probably know all about their achievements. If that person is famous, they probably have headlines that praise their victories or triumphs. You rarely hear about their struggles, but I promise you that they have failed early and often. When you're faced with adversity, remember that a smooth sea never made a skilled sailor.

Leadership is difficult. Plain and simple. But most people don't take leadership seriously until it's too late. You're different. You care about leadership. You sincerely want to make everyone around you better. After you put this book down, go out and practice leadership. The world needs more people like you. Enjoy it. I guarantee that you will look back that these experiences with fond eyes and you will be thankful that you started now, and not later.

Remember, you don't need to be the perfect leader that you imagine in your head, but you do need to be flexible enough to be the leader that your group needs.

SELF-PUBLISHING
SCHOOL

NOW IT'S YOUR TURN

Discover the EXACT 3-step blueprint you need to become a bestselling author in 3 months.

Self-Publishing School helped me, and now I want them to help you with this FREE WEBINAR!

Even if you're busy, bad at writing, or don't know where to start, you CAN write a bestseller and build your best life.

With tools and experience across a variety niches and professions, Self-Publishing School is the only resource you need to take your book to the finish line!

DON'T WAIT

Watch this FREE WEBINAR now, and

Say "YES" to becoming a bestseller:

https://xe172.isrefer.com/go/affegwebinar/bookbrosinc6446/

Special Thanks to:

- Susana Mota
- Janie Lawson
- Tatiana Garcia
- Danny Briseno
- Adam Cruz
- Bryan A Jimenez
- Olga Garcia
- Sean Urciuoli
- NaLayah D Hatton
- Charlie Vasquez
- Jorge Molina
- Marlene Molina
- April Wells
- Amy De Jong
- Devon Post
- Daniel McNelis
- Grace Lemen
- Conner Post
- Angela Kaleta
- Garrett Barnes
- Jacinda Lubarski
- Julie Molina
- Bambi
- Elisa Ramos
- Keland Hill
- Kat Dant
- Abigail Jimenez
- Toria Soto
- Colleen Spork
- Jupe Townsend
- Tommy Yu (Brunson)
- Michael Martinez
- Gena Soto
- Crystal Deel
- Jess Ramos
- Sarah Blessing
- Katrina Molina

CPSIA information can be obtained
at www.ICGtesting.com
Printed in the USA
LVHW050012100719
623642LV00007B/31